Hot Springs
and Pools
of the Northwest

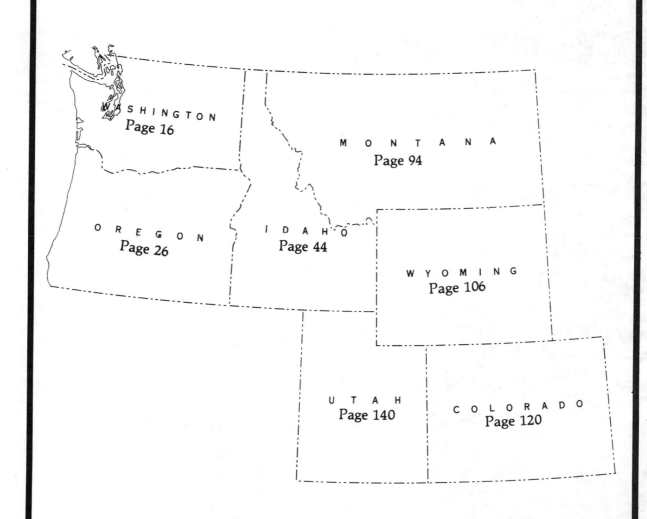

WASHINGTON
Page 16

MONTANA
Page 94

OREGON
Page 26

IDAHO
Page 44

WYOMING
Page 106

UTAH
Page 140

COLORADO
Page 120

Hot Springs and Pools of the Northwest

COLORADO, OREGON, WASHINGTON,
IDAHO, UTAH, MONTANA, WYOMING

JAYSON LOAM

CAPRA PRESS
Santa Barbara
1980

Grateful
Acknowledgements
To:

My sons Mel and Randy for their timely advice
and support; Terry and Janice for the use of their
van; National Forest and National Park personnel
for their courtesy and cooperation; the hot spring
soakers who agreed to be in the photographs; the
resort owners for their hospitality; Jeanne and
Wade for their technical support; and the Department of Energy for inviting me to attend the
Geothermal Conference in Salt Lake City.

Art Direction by Haaga Design Studio
Typesetting by Heath and Associates
Photographs and maps by Jayson Loam

Copyright © 1980 by Jayson Loam
All rights reserved
Manufactured in the United States of America.

Camera work by Santa Barbara Photoengraving.
Printed and bound by R. R. Donnelley & Sons.

Library of Congress Cataloging
in Publication Data
Loam, Jayson.
    Hot springs & pools of the Northwest.
    1. Health resorts, watering-places, etc.
    — Northwestern States — Directories.
    2. Hot springs — Northwestern States
    — Guide-books. I. Title
RA807.N93L62   613'.122'025795   79-27477
ISBN 9-88496-143-5

CAPRA PRESS
Post Office Box 2068
Santa Barbara, California 93120

Dedicated to Bubbles, a gutsy and tender lady, who posesses flexibility, that precious attribute of a truly enjoyable traveling companion.

Foreword

In this second volume on hot springs Jayson Loam takes me, a Californian, beyond my familiar haunts into Colorado and the Northwest where I have never been. I have long fantasized about the terrain in these rugged states, from coastal forests to the spewing geysers of Yellowstone, but I never found the occasion to get there. Now that I am shown where the hot springs are I feel it's high time to *make* the occasion. This book covers a vast territory, much of it sparsely populated, where I expect outdoor soaking will be a more solitary and meditative experience.

Compared to Loam's first volume, which dealt with hot springs in California and the Southwest, this one is organized more as a guide book with less emphasis on a few favored springs and spas. In these pages more than 200 locations are described and photographed, with maps wherever needed, making this a comprehensive directory.

When it comes to appreciations, Loam certainly has his bents and makes no bones about them. We soon know he loves nothing more than "an idyllic, tree-shaded natural hot mineral pool" where he can peel off his clothes and skinny dip to his heart's content. We also realize how earnest he is about urging practical applications of geothermal power. He also gives space to other's perceptions, however. Mainly, he brings us hard-won information in an orderly manner, shows us which springs are where, and what to expect when we arrive. It's a diligent compilation with enough unabashed enthusiasm to inspire us to be there, without beclouding the reality of the place. By this I mean the amenities, public conveniences or lack of them, temperature of the water, and local attitudes towards nudity.

Although Loam doesn't use a star rating system, I think of these directories as Michelin Guides to the hot springs and pools of the whole, vast, wild, thermal West.

— Leon Elder,
author of *HOT TUBS*

Contents

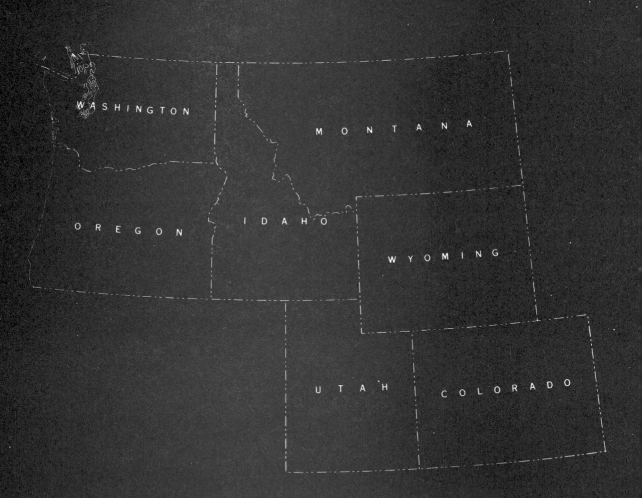

Mountains, Trees and Mineral Water

The very word NORTHWEST can conjure up images of snow-clad peaks, cascading rivers, lush forests, clean air, spectacular sunsets and the associated joys of skiing, fishing, boating, hiking, riding, looking, smelling, listening and feeling. The words HOT SPRING can then add images of an idyllic natural soaking pool of comforting and relaxing liquid warmth, sending up wisps of steam into magical surroundings.

For people who like such images, and the reality to match, the good news is that there are really a few such hot mineral pools in the northwestern United States, such as Vulcan Hot Springs in Idaho on the front cover of this book, and Valley View Hot Springs in Colorado on the back cover. For people who avoid muddy natural bottoms, rugged hiking trails, dusty roads and the total absence of privacy, toilets or showers, the good news is that these northwestern states also have dozens of commercial hot spring resorts which surround their natural mineral water with all the modern conveniences. The Northwest is a most rewarding area for people with a wide variety of tastes and preferences for places to peacefully soak their bodies in hot water.

The purpose of this book is to help people find these places and to make informed choices from the many alternatives available. The one thing all hot springs have in common

CAPRA HOT SPRINGS . . . . page 35

11

is water; beyond that there is an incredible variety which obviously did not come from an assembly line. Consider some of the more obvious aspects:

Water Temperature

Natural mineral water can vary from below 52 degrees, which is perfect for raising fish, to more than 300 degrees, the temperature of superheated steam used to generate electricity.

Mineral Content

In some cases, the dissolved minerals in water are colorless, odorless and tasteless. In other cases, the content is so caustic that it corrodes away heavy metal pipe in less than six months, or is so concentrated that giant mounds of minerals are deposited each year as the outflowing water cools. Some waters offend the nose with the rotten egg odor of H_2S, while others taste like a freshly opened bottle of soda pop. Most have invisible concentrations of minerals which can only be identified through laboratory analysis. They are all different to some degree, which leads to extended arguments between resorts over whose analysis is the best.

Pattern of Emergence

Only a few geothermal outflows take the form of geysers, which have alternating periods of discharge and rest, while some other outflows resemble cold water springs. Most hot springs have some bubbles or turbulence some of the time. Depending on the geology of the area, hot mineral water may spurt out of cracks in a rocky cliff, or cascade down a river bank, or trickle over the lip of its own mineral deposits, or well up in a gravel wash, or burble up through the sandy bottom of a river, or even boil out of colorful mud pots.

Pools and Ponds

Only a few hot springs have just the right temperature, mineral content and rate of flow to produce and fill a self-built "hot pot" suitable for immersing the human body. Also, only a few sites can offer a rock pool carved by surface run-off water which is filled by geothermal water at the ideal temperature for people soaking. Usually, mineral water is too hot to touch when it flows from the ground, but the cooling process starts immediately when it makes contact with the air. Human ingenuity then uses rocks, logs and mud to build cooling ponds, or a dam at that place where the geothermal run-off has cooled to approximately 100 degrees. Because most undeveloped hot springs in the Northwest flow only a short distance to a surface stream, the most prevalent form of temperature control is a primitive rock pool along the edge of the stream. Depending on the terrain, either the hot mineral water or the cold surface water is diverted from the pool as needed to control the temperature of the soaking water within.

Constructed pools have used redwood, cedar, mahogany, cement block, natural stone, concrete, plaster, fiberglass and acryllic. They vary in size from a one-person therapy tub to Olympic-size swimming pools and larger.

Swimming pool health standards of all states require that regularly tested water

BELKNAP HOT SPRINGS . . . . page 35

samples may not exceed some very low level of bacteria count. Furthermore, these Health Department standards (written primarily for city swimming pools which recycle their water), also require automatic chlorination of the water to certain minimum levels.

Some fortunate hot spring owners have a mineral content which permits adding chlorine without turning the water black. Other fortunate hot springs owners live in states which permit pool operation without chlorination as long as a minimum rate of constant flow-through is maintained. Then there are the unfortunate hot spring owners who cannot do either of the above. They must fill their swimming pools with city water, and keep it chlorinated, drawing only the heat from mineral water.

Buildings

You will find minimum bathhouses consisting of no more than a roofless fence built around a small rock-dammed hot spring flowing out of the ground at approximately 100 degrees. There are also resort complexes where one wing of the main building holds a larger-than-Olympic-size swimming pool, and there are establishments which pipe their geothermal water in from miles away. In

between there is a multitude of shapes and sizes of buildings, representing a wide variety of ideas of how to accommodate the customers drawn by the magic of hot water.

Laws, Rules and Customs

Laws regarding private property are similar from state to state: they all make trespassing on posted property a punishable crime. Therefore, the AQUA PAGES Directory does not include privately-owned hot springs which are posted or otherwise identified as being unavailable to the public. Even if some local citizens have been known to sneak into such a hot spring, that site has been omitted from the Directory because this book is not intended to steer readers into situations where they are liable to be arrested or shot.

When it comes to clothing, or lack thereof, each state has its own laws on the subject, different hot springs establishments have different rules, and the primitive hot spring sites have different customs. Here again, the purpose of this book is to provide reliable information which will keep you from being arrested or otherwise hassled. Most commercial establishments require bathing suits. Only a small minority of these tolerate late-nite unofficial skinny-dipping. Several establishments have an official clothing-optional policy, sometimes applicable only in the pool area. A very few places flatly prohibit bathing suits in the pools.

Unimproved (or unattended) hot springs may be privately or publicly owned, and there may be some uncertainty about the applicable laws and/or rules. The absence of a sign saying "No Nude Bathing" does not tell you whether or not such a sign was torn down before you arrived on the scene. You may be tempted to imitate whatever clothing policy was being followed by those who arrived before you, but it is quite possible that they are no better informed than you are about

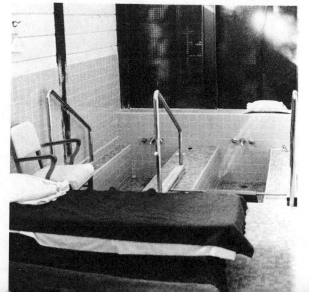

what the laws and rules actually are. It is easy to say "When in doubt, wear a bathing suit" yet some people consider that a last resort, not a first course of action.

There is one policy which will minimize the risk of adverse reactions, no matter what the laws, rules and customs are: go by mutual consent of those present. If you happen to prefer skinny-dipping, ask the people present when you arrive if you have their consent for you to soak *au naturel*. Then be sure to ask all later arrivals if you have their consent as well. Of course, mutual agreement to break an anti-nudity law cannot protect any of you from being technically in violation, but the chances of being in big trouble are greatly reduced when no one is complaining that you offended them against their will.

At some small remote hot springs, with and without bathhouse walls, there is a local custom of waiting outside (or in the parking area) until the current occupants leave. Obviously, this custom is based on the assumption that the current occupants are skinny-dipping and would not want strangers as company. In the winter this can cause people to wait in line in the snow while one group has the hot pool to themselves. No doubt it would be wise for you to follow this custom when you encounter it, but why not at least give the current bathers an opportunity to invite you to join them, by your letting them know that is your preference. Even if you get a "no" you are no worse off than if you did not give them a chance to say "yes."

Gas-heated City Water Pools

As part of this book's goal to guide you to all the places where you may put your body in hot water, the AQUA PAGES Directory includes the motels, hotels and RV Parks which offer hot pools to their registered guests. Also included are more complete details about the rapidly growing number of rent-a-tub establishments. For the city dwellers who choose not to make the trip to a hot spring, at least some aspects of the hot spring experience can be brought to town. When natural hot springs are not conveniently available, almost-as-good-as-the-real-thing is far better than no soak at all.

Geothermal Energy

Until recently, most government and media attention has been given to high temperature geothermal developments having the potential of producing electric power in large quantities. Now, with the price of natural gas and heating oil climbing daily, geothermal space and water heating programs are receiving increased emphasis. At first glance it might appear that none of the geothermal applications could have any significant relationship to the question of where people can go to soak in hot water, and it is true that the super-heated steam used in electric turbines is hardly suitable for human skin. However, some of the lower temperature (below boiling) appli-

TIME OUT BATHS . . . . page 127

cations have the potential for delivering large amounts of low-cost just-hot-enough mineral water in or near substantial population centers. Some day it might become possible to construct a dozen idyllic, tree-shaded, skinny-dipping mineral water hot pools on a downtown roof-top, available for rent by the hour.

The Department of Energy is doing its bureaucratic best to promote the utilization of both high temperature and low temperature geothermal energy, along with other alternate energy sources in this country. Each of the seven Northwest states included in this book has a contract with DOE to locate and assess all of its geothermal resources. Each state also has a separate contract to make area studies and site specific plans designed to accelerate the use of such resources by institutions, industry, agriculture and local government agencies. At the beginning of 1980 these seven states had 11 of the 23 Western demonstration projects funded by DOE. The individual projects will be described at the end of each state chapter.

Generally speaking, it is unlikely that geothermal applications to institutions, industry or agriculture will generate many hot pools for public soaking, primarily because of inconvenient locations. However, all of the local heating district projects offer interesting possibilities because ech one is specifically designed to deliver geothermal heat energy to a center of population. At some stage in the direct heating process, heat exchangers are used to transfer energy from the hot mineral water to circulating air (space heating) or to reservoir water (domestic hot water), or to other specialized commercial uses in the district. Experience has shown that it is not efficient to try to extract space and water heating energy from the hot mineral water once that mineral water has cooled to less than 115 degrees in the heat exchanger. At that point it becomes surplus mineral water

which will be piped back to a reinjection well, or possibly discarded directly to a storm sewer drain.

In either case, this water needs only a little more cooling to be just right for flowing through soaking pools, after which it can be sent on its way to reinjection or a storm drain. One of the aims of the Aqua Thermal Association is to help accomplish such a hot tub facility in connection with one or more of the geothermal heating districts.

The constantly escalating cost of fuel oil has also stimulated widespread interest in the production of methanol, the alcohol component in gasahol. Methanol production can be accomplished without geothermal energy, but the distilling process requires such a large amount of heat that geothermal offers an ideal low-cost source at suitable temperatures. Preliminary studies indicate that the best location for a methanol demonstration project is an area which has a high total tonnage of agricultural waste to feed into the distilling process, and substantial livestock herds which can be fed the nutritious dry-cake end product that is left after the methanol is distilled off. Some observers predict that the full application of geothermal sources to methanol production could save at least as much or more imported oil as will be saved by all of the geothermal electric production. We hope some of these methanol plants will include soaking pools for the enjoyment of their employees.

REGIONAL KEY MAP

● Unimproved Mineral Water Locations
■ Improved Mineral Water Locations
□ City Water Establishments

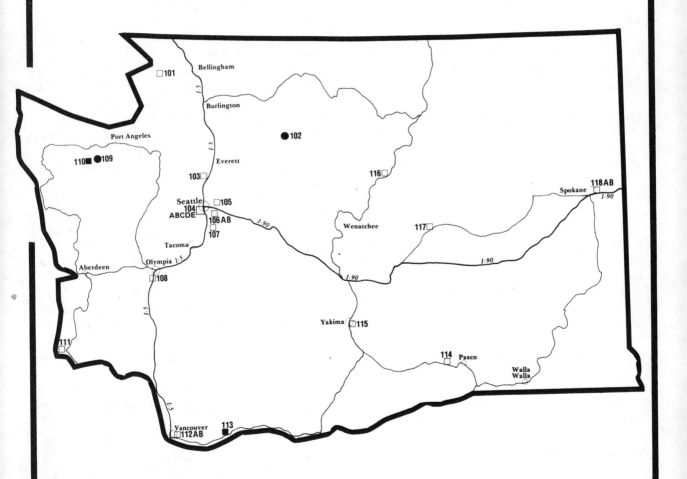

Each location has been assigned a location number,
and Directory listings have been arranged numerically.

WASHINGTON:

The Wettest
and the Coolest

There is rarely a lack of water in Washington, especially in the western portion. Nearly a thousand miles of shoreline and many counties get hundreds of inches of rainfall every years. At the same time, the very clouds which bring so much moisture also block out sunshine for weeks at a stretch. The end result is cold and damp as well as lush and green.

Coincidentally, Washington's shortage of solar energy is paralleled by a shortage of geothermal energy. Although the mountains contain several imposing extinct volcanoes, nearly all the volcanic heat from the earth's core seems to have retreated beyond the reach of surface water. Only a few scattered springs are accessible, and some of these flow too slowly to permit public use without creating a health hazard. A glance through the AQUA PAGES Directory shows there are more trailer parks with hot therapy pools than there are natural hot springs available to the public. In fact, the total of all kinds of geothermal phenomena, including hot gas fumaroles, is so small that a federally-funded energy task force is being forced to literally "beat the bushes" for remote geothermal springs that may have remained concealed by the under-brush for centuries.

Two of Washington's active hot springs lie within Olympic National Park, on the Olympic Peninsula. Both Sol Duc and

OLYMPIC HOT SPRINGS . . . . page 23

Olympic Hot Springs were owned and developed by private interests from the 30s to the 50s. Sol Duc, with an aged collection of cabins and buildings, is only open during the Memorial Day-Labor Day summer season. Olympic Hot Springs ceased commercial operations in the 60s, was purchased by the National Park Service, and then subsequently cleared of all buildings. These two natural attractions are good examples of the management problems being faced by all agencies, (federal, state and county) responsible for hot springs on public lands, especially those with a short visitor season.

OLYMPIC HOT SPRINGS . . . . page 23

At Sol Duc the Park Service has the problem of providing clean, well-maintained facilities at reasonable fees in the face of inflated construction costs and government budget cuts. At Olympic Hot Springs, where buildings no longer exist, the problems are a little different. The National Park Service issued a "Voluntary Information and Public Input Sheet" on the Olympic Hot Springs. They described the spring as "a series of small springs rising along fissures in the underlying sedimentary rocks. The springs apparently receive part of their water supply from rain and melting snow which seep through cracks in the sedimentary rocks to an unknown depth where they mingle with water and gases coming from cooling volcanic rocks."

The Park Service memo goes on to say,

> Tradition has it that the Olympic Hot Springs were first discovered in September, 1892, but the finder did not stay, for he thought that the mountain was going to explode. At that time, the springs were seeps in a steep-sloped forest along Boulder Creek. The terraces and enlarged springs which are found there now are probably man-made. The springs were rediscovered on June 25, 1907 by Billy Everett, a local man who explored the Olympics extensively. In 1907, a trail from the Elwha was slashed, but a road was not completed until 1930. Everett and his wife built a cedar cabin in 1907, followed by the first family pool in 1910 and improved in 1916. The year 1920 brought a new lodge, and by the early 1930's the resort was booming. Over the years, facilities and public use declined.
>
> In order to meet changing public health standards, the National Park Service in 1955 asked that the hot mineral water be replaced with fresh water. With declining revenues, the resort was closed and purchased by the Service in 1966. A heavy snowfall shortly thereafter collapsed the remaining structures.
>
> For the past few years, the use of the hot springs have involved a considerable increase of illegal activities such as underage drinking, use of drugs, public nudity, nude bathing, theft, and poor public hygiene. The increasing amount of human waste and litter have been a major concern to park management.
>
> The Service must, and will, enforce the law in the area and illegal acts will not be permitted. Likewise, we are sincerely interested in protecting the park visitors and increasing their enjoyment of the park.
>
> We are considering several management alternatives and would like your ideas and comments. If you wish to help, please provide your comments to us in writing.

The Aqua Thermal Association made the following suggestions and observations in a letter dated September 27, 1979:

> Unquestionably, a majority of vacationing families want the familiar facilities and conventional behavior of a developed commercial resort, including a chlorinated swimming pool, bathing suits, dressing rooms, flush toilets, a snack bar and a recreation room with electronic game machines. Usually such families have little or no interest in mineral water, per se. On the other hand there is a rapidly growing minority (including some families) who prefer a quiet soak in hot mineral water, without swim suits, in primitive natural surroundings, and who are willing to spend the time and energy of a long hike to enjoy such an experience. Both groups deserve to be accomodated, but obviously not at the same hot spring.
>
> At a developed hot spring resort such as Sol Duc, the day-to-day administration can be delegated to an operator who leases the ground and improvements, and who has employees to open and close the premises, supervise dress and behavior codes, and when necessary, call in peace officers to quell excess rowdiness. At a primitive site, such as Olympic Hot Springs, there is no commercial operator and it is not practical for you to station a full-time Ranger at the location.
>
> It is my observation that several National Forest Districts with primitive hot spring locations have eliminated or minimized most of the problems by making the primitive hot spring site truly *remote*, and by designating it for day use only. This is accomplished by keeping the nearest road, parking area or campground at least ½ mile away, connected only by a not-too-easy trail. Minimum privies are provided near the hot springs but a litter can is provided only at the trailhead. Such a policy recognizes that the hot springs enthusiast is a form of wilderness hiker, who does not expect or want the comforts or dress limitations of a conventional resort, and who is as conscientious as most back-packers about caring for the cleanliness of a naturally beautiful site.
>
> In my opinion the geography of Olympic Hot Springs is a direct cause of most of the present problems. There is now a parking area and a campground within 100 yards of the springs:
>
> (a) During the dalight hours this parking area attracts vacationing couples and families who take a short "sightseeing" walk down the

path toward the hot springs, become offended at the sight of nude bathers, and complain loudly to your office that "somebody ought to do something!" In the meantime, that same nudity is a non-problem among the hot spring bathers themselves. Actually, the Federal Regulations now make it clear that there must be an offended observer willing to sign a complaint with a magistrate before nudity can be a cause for punitive Ranger action.

(b) During the evening hours this parking area attracts the compulsive party-time drinkers and dopers. Furthermore, the adjoining campground justifies overnight parking, so there is no time limit on the partying, which just increases the probability of irresponsible behavior.

Relocating the parking area, road and campground at least ½ mile away, and posting the hot springs for daytime use only would have the following effects:

1. Eliminate the "short walk" tourists and families who are now offended by the nude bathers.

2. Discourage nearly all of the compulsive party crowd, who would face a ½ mile hike away from their precious "wheels" and then face another ½ mile hike back when it got dark. (Yes, a Ranger will need to make a midnight sweep through the hot springs area several times a week for a while until word gets around about what a bummer it is to carry sleeping gear down a dark trail at 1 o'clock in the morning.) The party crowd will simply choose to go to other places which are more convenient and comfortable for partying. There is some reason to believe that most of the theft problems will go with them.

3. Substantially reduce the total quantity of people who go to the location each day, thereby keeping a lot of potential litter from ever getting to the area.

4. Attract the hot spring enthusiasts who do cherish such a beautiful natural setting, and who make a habit of carrying out extra litter in addition to what they brought in.

One of the hot spring bathers I met put it in these words, "Soaking in a primitive hot spring surrounded by natural beauty is such a rare and valuable experience that it should not be wasted on irresponsible people who bring artificial highs, loud rock music and excess litter wherever they

OLYMPIC HOT SPRINGS . . . . page 23

go." I agree with this sentiment, and respectfully suggest that you retain the primitive status of Olympic Hot Springs while changing the public access to the area in the manner described above.

Jayson Loam
Executive Director

In the months since the preceding letter was mailed, the National Park Service has acknowledged its receipt, saying in part, "You offer some very positive suggestions for ways to reduce conflicts of varying uses. We will consider your recommendations as plans are prepared for the future use of this unique resource." As of Spring 1980, the new plans for Olympic Hot Springs had not been announced.

The National Park Service did issue a press release announcing new plans for Sol Duc Hot Springs, including "warming the cold pool, a new hot pool and bathhouse, a redesigned lodge with food service and store, trailer hook-ups and a new picnic area. The season will also be extended in accordance with the finances available. New sources of hot spring water make it possible to heat the buildings with geothermal energy."

Geothermal Energy

Thanks to the scarcity of geothermal resources, neither high-temperature electricity generating projects nor low-temperature demonstration projects exist in Washington. However, feasibility studies have begun at Sol Duc Hot Springs in Olympic National Park, and in the city of North Bonneville. Preliminary studies have also been started on the possible use of warm-water-plus-heat-pump applications in Ephrata School District and in the Yakima School District.

SOL DUC HOT SPRINGS . . . . page 24

The following codes were used in the preparation of listings and maps on the following pages.

NATURAL MINERAL WATER LOCATIONS ARE SET IN BOLD TYPE — like this
GAS HEATED CITY WATER LOCATIONS ARE SET IN REGULAR TYPE — like this

PR = *Tubs or pools for rent, by hour, day or treatment.*
MH = *Rooms or cabins for rent by day, week or month.*
RV = *Vehicle spaces for rent by day, week, month, or year.*

Open all year means that there are no doors or gates closed during a part of the year. However, snow or high water may temporarily make the location inaccessible.

——————— **Paved highway**
— — — — **Gravel or dirt road**
············· **Hiking trail**
▲ **Campground**

#101   ROSARIO RESORT HOTEL
(San Juan Islands)   (206) 376-2222
Eastsound, WA 98245   Therapy Pool   MH

#102   KENNEDY HOT SPRINGS   (see Map)
In the Glacier Peak Wilderness Area

A remote hot spring which has been dug out and lined with cedar boards to make a 4' by 5' soaking pool. Located in a rugged canyon on the White Chuck River. For overnite stays a permit must be obtained from a Mt. Baker · Snoqualmie National Forest Ranger Station. Elevation 3,800 ft. Open all year.

Natural Mineral Water flows out of the ground at 96 degrees directly into the pool. There is no posted clothing policy, which leaves it up to the mutual consent of those present.

No facilities on the premises. 5 miles to campground at trailhead. 30 miles to cafe, grocery store, service station, motel and RV hookups. 60 miles to public bus.

Source maps: Mt. Baker · Snoqualmie National Forest; USGS · Glacier Park and Pugh Mountain, Washington.

#103   BEST WESTERN LANDMARK INN
4300 200th St. SW   (206) 775-7447
Lynwood, WA 98036   Hydrojet Pool   MH

#104A   BEST WESTERN EXECUTIVE INN
200 Taylor Ave. N.   (206) 628-9444
Seattle, WA 98109   Rooms with Hydrojet Pool   MH

#104B   BEST WESTERN LOYAL INN
2301 8th Ave.   (206) 682-0200
Seattle, WA 98121   Therapy Pool   MH

#104C   RODEWAY INN
12501 Aurora Ave. N   (206) 364-7771
Seattle, WA 98133   Therapy Pool   MH

#104D   BEST WESTERN JET INN
3000 S. 176th St.   (206) 246-9110
Seattle, WA 98188   Therapy Pool   MH

#104E   VANCE AIRPORT INN
18220 Pacific Hwy S.   (206) 246-5535
Seattle, WA 98118   Therapy Pool   MH

#105   TRAILER INNS
                                      (206) 747-9181
Bellevue, WA 98009   Therapy Pool   RV

#106A   AQUA BARN RANCH CAMPGROUND
                                      (206) 255-4618
Renton, WA 98055   Therapy Pool   RV

#106B   DOUBLETREE INN SOUTHCENTER
205 Strander Blvd.   (206) 246-8220
Renton, WA 98188   Rooms with thermal bath   MH

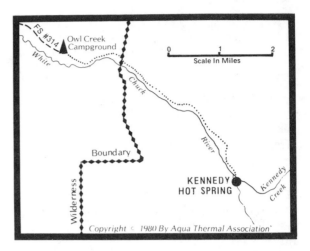

#107   BEST WESTERN PONY SOLDIER MOTEL
1233 N. Central   (206) 852-7224
Kent, WA 98031   Therapy Pool   MH

#108   VANCE TYEE MOTOR INN
500 Tyee Dr.   (206) 352-0511
Tumwater, WA 98362 Cabana units with hydropool   MH

#109 OLYMPIC HOT SPRINGS (see map)
Near the town of Port Angelus

Several primitive springs in Olympic National Park, on the side of a steep ravine, surrounded by lush rain forest greenery. Elevation 1600 ft. Open all year except when road closed by snow.

Natural Mineral Water flows out of the ground at 100 to 110 degrees. Volunteers have built primitive rock soaking pools below the spring flows, holding the water in the 95 to 105 degree range. There is no posted clothing policy, which leaves it up to the mutual consent of those present.

No services on the premises. A tents-only campground is 200 yards away. 8 miles to cafe and grocery store. 20 miles to motel, service station, RV facilities and public bus.

Source maps: Olympic National Park; USGS - Mt. Carrie, Washington.

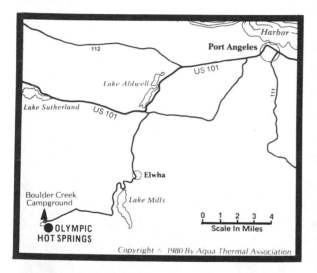

Copyright © 1980 By Aqua Thermal Association

OLYMPIC HOT SPRINGS: *The pipe is all there is left of the old resort buildings.*

In this larger pool the water cools down to about 95 degrees, ideal for a long soak.

Each of the several springs along the canyon feeds a separate small soaking pool.

#110 SOL DUC RESORT
Star Route 1, Box 11   *(no phone)*
Port Angelus, WA 98362   *PR + RV + MH*

Older commercial summer resort in Olympic National Park, surrounded by miles of lush rain forest greenery. Elevation 1600 ft. Open Memorial Day through Labor Day.

Natural Mineral Water flows out of the ground at 128 degrees. One outdoor soaking pool (no chlorine) maintained at 104 degrees. Six individual tubs in private rooms, controllable to 110 degrees.

The outdoor swimming pool contains fresh water, chlorinated, with an average temperature of 75 degrees. Bathing suits required, except in individual rooms.

Rooms, cabins, restaurant, grocery store, full hook-up RV spaces, tent spaces and picnic grounds on the premises. VISA and MC accepted. 14 miles to service station. 40 miles to public bus.

From US 101, 4 miles west of Fairholm, take Soleduck River road 14 miles south to resort.

#111 CHATAQUA LODGE
205 W. 14th St. N   *(206) 642-2244*
Long Beach, WA 98631   *Therapy Pool MH*

#112A SHILO INN - HAZEL DELL
13206 Hwy 99   *(206) 573-0511*
Vancouver, WA 98665   *Therapy Pool MH*

#112B SHILO INN - DOWNTOWN
401 E. 13th St.   *(206) 696-0411*
Vancouver, WA 98660   *Therapy Pool MH*

▲
▼ *SOL DUC RESORT: Both of the pools are drained & deserted after Labor Day. This historic resort, surrounded by a lush rain forest, is due for major improvements.*

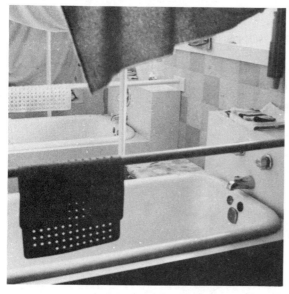

MOFFET'S HOT SPRING RESORT: *Single tubs are offered in separate bathhouses. Tree-shaded RV park is just beyond main building and large outdoor swimming pool.*

#113   MOFFETT'S HOT SPRING RESORT
Box 116   **(509) 427-8221**
North Bonneville, WA 98639   **PR + RV**

Older resort with RV facilities. Wooded grounds are less than a mile from the Columbia River and Bonneville Dam. Elevation 400 ft. Open all year.

Natural Mineral Water flows out of the ground at 96 degrees. Outdoor swimming pool maintained at 85 degrees. Five indoor individual tubs in private rooms, controllable to 110 degrees. Bathing suits required except in private rooms.

Full hook-up RV spaces, tent spaces and picnic area on the premises. No credit cards accepted. 1 mile to cafe and grocery store. 3 miles to motel, service station and public bus.

From Interstate 80N, cross the Columbia River on the Bridge of the Gods, then 3 miles west on Washington Route 14. Follow "Recreation Area" signs 1 mile north to resort.

#114   HOLIDAY INN
1515 George Washington Way   **(509) 946-4121**
Richland, WA 99352   *Whirlpool   MH*

#115   TRAILER INNS
                                  (509) 452-9561
Yakima, WA 98901   *Therapy Pool   RV*

#116   CAMPBELL'S LODGE AND COTTAGES
Box 278   **(509) 682-2561**
Chelan, WA 98816   *Therapy Pool   MH*

#117   PATTI - O - PARK
                                    (509) 246-1121
Soap Lake, WA 98851   *Therapy Pool   RV*

#118A   TRAVELODGE - RIVER INN
N. 700 Division St.   **(509) 326-5577**
Spokane, WA 99202   *Therapy Pool   MH*

#118B   TRAILER INNS
                                  (509) 535-1811
Spokane, WA 99204   *Therapy Pool   RV*

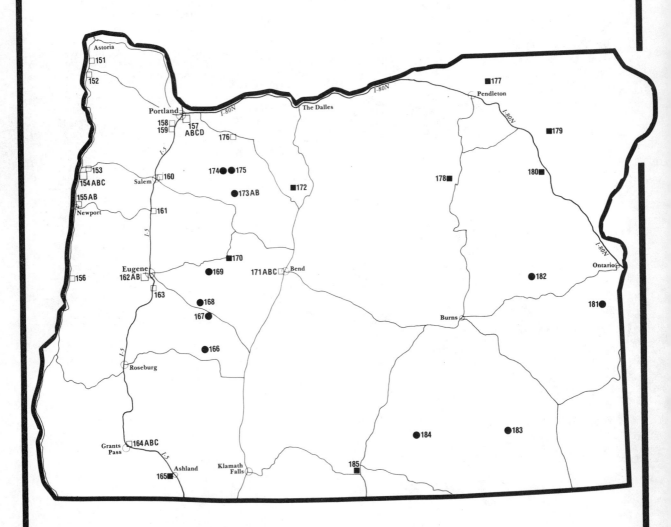

REGIONAL KEY MAP

● Unimproved Mineral Water Locations
■ Improved Mineral Water Locations
□ City Water Establishments

Astoria
□151
□152
Portland
158 □157
159 □ABCD
□176
□153
154 ABC
155 AB
Newport
□160
Salem
□161
174 ●●175
●173 AB
■172
I-80N
The Dalles
I-80N
■177
Pendleton
■179
178■
180■
□170
169●
171 ABC□—Bend
Eugene
162 AB□
□156
□163
168●
167●
166●
Roseburg
182●
Ontario
181●
Burns
184●
183●
Grants Pass
□164 ABC
Ashland
165■
Klamath Falls
185■

Each location has been assigned a location number,
and Directory listings have been arranged numerically.

OREGON:

Brave Nude World — Sometimes

In a nationwide "free beaches" publication, Oregon is identified as the most liberated of states, because nudity is legal everywhere except where municipalities or city-counties have legislated against it. This permissiveness is reflected in the clothing policies in effect at hot pools, although no one should expect to encounter an idyllic, tree-shaded skinny-dipping hot mineral pool every few miles.

Actually, most of the geothermal springs are privately owned and commercially operated, usually requiring bathing suits to be worn everywhere except in private rooms. The family-oriented community plunges strictly adhere to this policy, but some resorts are responding to public demand by unofficially tolerating late night skinny-dipping and/or nude co-ed use of the sauna. These semi-conservative locations are not identified in the AQUA PAGES Directory because the permissive policies are unofficial. A discreet inquiry is recommended.

A few commercial resorts are making an up-front effort to accommodate both the older conservative clientele and the younger more liberal customers. For example, Breitenbush Hot Springs (Lower Camp) has two bathhouses, each containing a large soaking pool where bathing suits are prohibited. Before 7 P.M. the traditional segregation of men and women in the two bathhouses is maintained. After 7 P.M., both bathhouses become

MCCREDIE HOT SPRINGS . . . . page 32

27

available for co-ed use, and bathing suits are still prohibited in both soaking pools.

Some privately-owned hot springs are so remote that it is not practical to operate them commercially, and most of these are unfenced and unposted. In the absence of posted clothing requirements, and with no staff to enforce any requirement, the question of clothing is left to the mutual consent of those present. Clothing-optional is the usual choice.

Within National Forests, federal policy permits nudity everywhere except in those areas where it has been prohibited by the local Forest Supervisor. This confluence of state and federal permissiveness is most visible at McCredie Hot Springs, an easily accessible skinny-dipping geothermal pool, just a few yards off a paved highway. According to the local ranger station, they get few complaints about the nude bathing because most families who go there simply join the group in the large soaking pools on a clothing-optional basis.

Actually, Oregon does have a few of those idyllic hot mineral pools, tucked away at the end of hiking trails on National Forest property. Little known, and seldom used (except on weekends), Cougar Reservoir, Umpqua and Wall Creek Hot Springs have a picture post-card quality which justifies the dusty travel over gravel roads and hoofing along winding forest trails.

In marked contrast are the gas-heated city water hot pools offered by motels, hotels and RV parks. They are usually indoors, available only for communal use by registered guests, and bathing suits are usually required. Here again, discreet inquiries are advised to determine whether a clothing-optional policy is officially or unofficially observed. Oregon law books may be liberated on the subject of nudity, but the individual resort (whether mineral water or city water) must keep the customers happy. Not all of the customers share identical attitudes towards clothing, or the absence thereof.

AUSTIN HOT SPRINGS . . . . page 39

Geothermal Energy

Only a handful of existing commercial hot springs resorts have had the foresight to use geothermal energy for heating buildings and domestic water supplies. However, all resorts with plans for new construction have included designs for such energy conservation systems.

A DOE-funded industrial project near Ontario is designed to demonstrate the application of geothermal heat to the processing of potatoes. In Klamath Falls, dozens of homes and buildings at Oregon Institute of Technology have been geothermally heated for years, with each property owner drilling his own well into the large hot water reservoir underlying much of the city. A DOE institutional project for the Klamath County YMCA involves the drilling of such a well, with the potential for supplying all of the Y's heating needs, including heating the indoor swimming pool. Another DOE demonstration project in Klamath Falls is designed to provide heat to 14 city, state and federal buildings, with built-in expansion capacity to eventually supply many of the nearby buildings.

The following codes were used in the preparation of listings and maps on the following pages.

NATURAL MINERAL WATER LOCATIONS ARE SET IN BOLD TYPE — like this
GAS HEATED CITY WATER LOCATIONS ARE SET IN REGULAR TYPE — like this

PR = *Tubs or pools for rent, by hour day or treatment.*
MH = *Rooms or cabins for rent by day, week or month.*
RV = *Vehicle spaces for rent by day, week, month, or year.*

Open all year means that there are no doors or gates closed during a part of the year. However, snow or high water may temporarily make the location inaccessible.

——————— **Paved highway**
— — — — **Gravel or dirt road**
. . . . **Hiking trail**
▲ **Campground**

#151   BEST WESTERN SEASHORE RESORT MOTEL
60 N. Promenade, Banks   (503) 738-6368
Seaside, OR 97138   Whirlpool   MH

#152   BEST WESTERN SURFSAND RESORT HOTEL
Box 547   (503) 436-2274
Cannon Beach, OR 97110   Therapy Pools   MH

#153   PIXIELAND TRAILER PARK
                                      (503) 994-3646
Otis, OR 97368   Therapy Pool   RV

#154A   INTERNATIONAL DUNES OCEANFRONT RESORT
Box 954   (503) 994-3655
Lincoln City, OR 97367   Therapy Pool   MH

#154B   SEA GYPSY MOTEL
145 NW Inlet Ave.   (503) 994-5266
Lincoln City, OR 97367   Therapy Pool   MH

#154C   SURFTIDES BEACH RESORT
2945 NW Jetty Ave.   (503) 994-2191
Lincoln City, OR 97367   Therapy Pool   MH

#155A   EMBARCADERO MARINA RESORT
1000 SE Bay Blvd.   (503) 265-8521
Newport, OR 97365   Whirlpool   MH

#155B   INTERNATIONAL DUNES OCEANFRONT MOTEL
536 SW Elizabeth Ave.   (503) 265-7701
Newport, OR 97365   Whirlpool   MH

#156   DRIFTWOOD SHORES RESORT INN
88416 First Ave.   (503) 997-8263
Florence, OR 97439   Therapy Pools   MH

#157A   BEST WESTERN KINGS WAY INN
420 NE Holladay Ave.   (503) 233-6331
Portland, OR 97232   Therapy Pool   MH

#157B   PORTLAND MARRIOTT HOTEL
1401 S.W. Front Ave.   (503) 226-7600
Portland, OR 97201   Hydrotherapy Pool   MH

#157C   COSMOPOLITAN AIRTEL
6221 NE 82nd Ave.   (503) 255-6511
Portland, OR 97220   Hot Mineral Bath   MH

#157D   RODEWAY INN CHUMAREE
NE 82nd & Sandy Blvd.   (503) 256-4111
Portland, OR 97220   Suites with whirlpool   MH

#158   BEST WESTERN VIPS MOTOR INN
17993 SW Lower Boones Ferry Rd.   (503) 620-2030
Tigard, OR 97223   Rooms with Hydrojet Pool   MH

#159   RODEWAY INN - PORTLAND SOUTHWEST
17835 SW Hazelfern Rd.   (503) 620-3460
Tualatin, OR 97062   Hydrojet Pool   MH

#160   BEST WESTERN NEW KINGS INN
3658 Market St. NE   (503) 581-1559
Salem, OR 97301   Therapy Pool   MH

#161   BEST WESTERN PONY SOLDIER INN
I-5 North Interchange   (503) 928-6322
Albany, OR 97321   Hydrojet Pool   MH

#162A   HOLIDAY INN
225 Coburg Road   (503) 342-5181
Eugene, OR 97401   Whirlpool   MH

#162B   VALLEY RIVER INN
1000 Valley River Way   (503) 687-0123
Eugene, OR 97401   Therapy Pools   MH

#163   KOA - SHERWOOD FOREST
                                      (503) 895-4110
Creswell, OR 97426   Therapy Pool   RV

#164A   BEST WESTERN RIVERSIDE MOTEL
971 S.E. Sixth St.   (503) 476-6873
Grants Pass, OR 97526   Therapy Pools   MH

#164B   ROYAL VUE MOTOR HOTEL
110 NE Morgan Lane   (503) 479-5381
Grants Pass, OR 97526   Therapy Pools   MH

#164C   SHILO INN
1880 NW Sixth St.   (503) 479-8391
Grants Pass, OR 97526   Therapy Pools   MH

#165   JACKSON HOT SPRINGS
2253 Hwy 99 North   (503) 482-3776
Ashland, OR 97520   PR + RV + MH

Older resort with public plunge. Elevation 1800 ft. Open all year.

Natural Mineral Water flows out of the ground at 86 degrees. Outdoor swimming pool (open June 1 to Sept. 30) maintained at 84 degrees in the summer and 78 degrees in winter. Two indoor individual tubs, adjustable to 110 degrees. Bathing suits required except in tub rooms.

Cabins, picnic grounds and full hook-up RV spaces available on the premises. VISA and MasterCharge accepted. 2 blocks to restaurant. ½ mile to service station. 2 miles to grocery store and public bus.

On US 99, two miles north of the town of Ashland.

#166 UMPQUA WARM SPRING   (see map)
40 miless northwest of Crater Lake National Park.

A semi-improved primitive hot spring on a wooded bluff in the Umpqua National Forest. Elevation 2800 ft. Open all year.

Natural Mineral Water flows out of the ground at 108 degrees into a partially enclosed pool carved out of the mineral formation, 100 feet above *Loafer Creek*. Pool temperature is controlled by diverting the flow of 108 degree water as desired. There is no clothing policy posted, leaving it up to the mutual consent of those present.

No facilities available on the premises. 25 miles to cafe, grocery store and service station. 45 miles to all other services, including public bus.

Source maps: Umpqua National Forest; USGS Toketee Falls, Oregon.

▼ *UMPQUA WARM SPRING: Over the years mineral deposits from the spring water have created this clearing in the dense woods. The rustic shelter was built over a soaking pool, with the open side providing a view of the other side of the canyon. The trail to the parking area is rugged but worth it.*

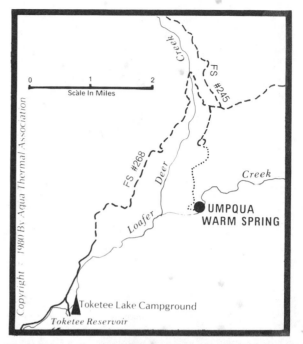

#167 MCCREDIE HOT SPRINGS   (see map)
Near the town of Oakridge, 50 miles southeast of Eugene.

Easily accessible primitive springs on the banks of Salt Creek, in the Willamette National Forest. Elevation 2000 ft. Open all year.

Natural Mineral Water flows out of the ground at 120 degrees into shallow rock and log pools, where it cools on its way to the creek. Although the pools are only 30 yards from the parking area they are not visible from the highway, so the local custom is clothing optional.

No services available on the premises. 11 miles to all services including public bus.

Source maps: Willamette National Forest; USGS Oakridge, Oregon.

◀ *MCCREDIE HOT SPRINGS: Water from the spring cools as it flows to the river.*

▲ *Adults as well as kids get to play in the mud; clothing is left to personal choice.*

▼ *A cooling dip in the river turns into a mother-in-the-middle family water fight.*

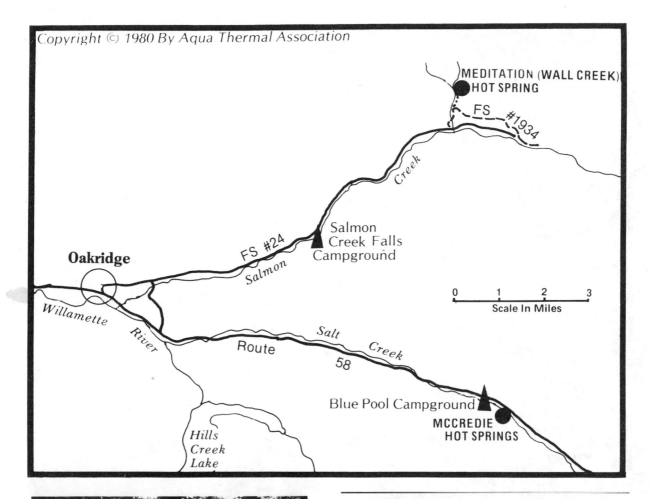

MEDITATION (WALL CREEK) HOT SPRING

FS #1934

Creek

FS #24

Salmon Creek Falls Campground

Salmon

Oakridge

Willamette

River

Route 58

Salt Creek

Blue Pool Campground

MCCREDIE HOT SPRINGS

Hills Creek Lake

0   1   2   3
Scale In Miles

#168 MEDITATION POOL (WALL CREEK)   (see map)
HOT SPRING
Near the town of Oakridge, 45 miles southeast of Eugene.

Primitive hot spring on the wooded bank of Wall Creek, in Willamette National Forest. Elevation 2200 ft. Open all year.

Natural Mineral Water flows out of the ground at 98 degrees directly into primitive rock pool, which maintains a temperature near 92 degrees, depending on wind and air temperature. The local custom is clothing optional.

No services on the premises. 4 miles to all services, including public bus.

Source maps: Willamette National Forest; USGS · Sardine Butte, Oregon.

MEDITATION POOL HOT SPRING: A short trail protects this idyllic spot from all traffic noises, leaving only the tumbling rush of a mountain stream. The water is not hot enough for therapy-type soaking but is ideal for effortless lolling.

OVEREXPOSURE! HAS NEGATIVE RESULTS

APPEARANCE
Please wear clothes by the road.
Don't offend other forest users.

CAPRA HOT SPRING: Sign at start of trail warns hot spring users to limit their nudity to the vicinity of the springs, where clothing optional is a tradition.

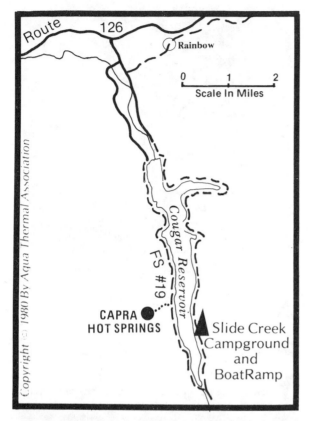

Route 126

Rainbow

0   1   2

Scale In Miles

Cougar Reservoir

FS #19

CAPRA
HOT SPRINGS

Slide Creek
Campground
and
BoatRamp

Copyright © 1980 By Aqua Thermal Association

▲ *CAPRA HOT SPRING: Log segment walks have been supplied by the Forest Service.*

▶ *BELKNAP HOT SPRING: 196 degree water flows through heat exchanger tank in foreground, where domestic and space-heating water absorb mineral water heat.*

#169   CAPRA (COUGAR RESERVOIR)   (see map) HOT SPRINGS
Near Cougar Reservoir, 50 miles east of Eugene

Primitive hot spring in a wooded ravine in the Willamette National Forest. Elevation 3000 ft. Open all year.

Natural Mineral Water flows out of the ground at 115 degrees, through a series of rock and log pools, gradually cooling to 90 degrees before joining a cold water creek. The local custom is clothing optional.

No services available on the premises. ¼ mile to parking area. 4 miles to campground. 8 miles to cafe, grocery store, service station, motel and overnight RV spaces. 50 miles to full hook-up RV spaces and public bus.

Source maps: Willamette National Forest.

#170   BELKNAP HOT SPRINGS
Box 1   (503) 822-3535
McKenzie Bridge, OR 97401   RV + MH

Modern commercial motel and RV park on the McKenzie River, surrounded by Willamette National Forest.

Natural Mineral Water flows out of the ground at 196 degree into a reservoir and heat exchanger. Two outdoor swimming pools, maintained at 102 degrees in winter and 93 degrees in summer, are available to registered motel and RV space guests only. Two motel rooms have jet pools controllable to 110 degrees, and 4 rooms have individual tubs controllable to 110 degrees. Bathing suits required except in rooms. All rooms and the domestic hot water system use geothermal heat from the heat exchanger.

Rooms, full hook-up RV spaces, tent spaces and fishing are available on the premises. VISA and Mastercharge accepted. 6 miles to cafe, grocery store and service station. 50 miles to public bus.

On Oregon Route 126, 6 miles east of the town of McKenzie Bridge. Follow signs.

#171A INN OF THE SEVENTH MOUNTAIN
Box 1207 Century Dr.   (503) 382-8711
Bend, OR 97701   Whirlpool   MH

#171B RIVERHOUSE MOTOR INN
3075 N. Hwy 97   (503) 389-3111
Bend, OR 97701   Hydrojet Pool   MH

#171C SUNRIVER RESORT
Sunriver   (503) 593-1246
Bend, OR 97701   Hot Tubs   MH

#172 KAH-NEE-TA VACATION RESORT VILLAGE
                                        (503) 553-1112
Warm Springs, OR 97761   PR + RV + MH

A major modern resort owned and operated by the
Confederated Tribes of the Warm Springs Indian Reservation. In these foothills on the east side of the Cascade
Mountains, the sun shines 340 days per year. Elevation
1500 ft. Open all year.

Natural Mineral Water flows out of the ground at 140
degrees. Outdoor swimming pool maintained at 100
degrees. Outdoor jet pool maintained at 105 degrees.
Men's and women's bathhouses have 5 individual soaking tubs controllable up to 110 degrees. Bathing suits
required except in bathhouses.

Room, cabins, teepees, restaurant, and full hook-up
RV spaces available on the premises. VISA, Mastercharge and American Express accepted. 11 miles to
grocery store, service station and public bus.

From US 26 in Warm Springs, follow signs 11 miles
northeast to resort.

▲ *KAH-NEE-TA VACATION VILLAGE:*
Real fires burn inside the rental teepees.

▶ *A fiberglass jet pool is in the deck*
adjoining the Olympic-size swimming pool

▼ *The feel of the wide open spaces has been*
preserved despite the modern conveniences.

36

37

▶ *AUSTIN HOT SPRINGS: A foot soak is enough for some people; others prefer a complete dunk.*

▼ *BREITENBUSH (UPPER CAMP): Miles of National Forest surround this historic hot spring resort.*

#173A   BREITENBUSH HOT SPRINGS (LOWER CAMP)
Box 588   (503) 854-3595
Detroit, OR 97342   PR + RV + MH

A rustic commercial resort on the wooded banks of the Breitenbush River, surrounded by the Willamette National Forest. Elevation 2000 ft. Open all year.

Natural Mineral Water flows out of the ground at 178 degrees. Two indoor soaking pools in men's and women's bathhouses maintained at 105 degrees. Communal co-ed use after 7 PM. Bathing suits not permitted in pools at any time. Major remodeling program may affect availability of pools; phone ahead to determine status of construction.

Cabins, grocery store and full hook-up RV spaces available on the premises. VISA and Mastercharge accepted. 10 miles to restaurant, service station and public bus.

From Oregon Route 22 in Detroit, follow signs northeast 10 miles on USFS road #224,

#173B   BREITENBUSH HOT SPRINGS (UPPER CAMP)
Box 578   no phone
Detroit, OR 97342

A non-commercial residential community on the banks of the Breitenbush River, surrounded by Willamette National Forest. Older lodge building and facilities being restored by residents, primarily for use by groups dealing with New Age concepts. Not open to the public, but a limited number of guest invitations are extended to those who inquire by mail. Elevation 2000 ft. Open all year.

Natural Mineral Water flows out of several springs at 180 degrees. Large outdoor pool is maintained at approximately 105 degrees. Clothing optional in pool area.

Cabins, tent spaces and communal meals available on the premises by prior arrangement. No credit cards. 11 miles to store, restaurant, service station and public bus.

From Oregon Route 22 in Detroit, follow signs 11 miles northeast on USFS road #224.

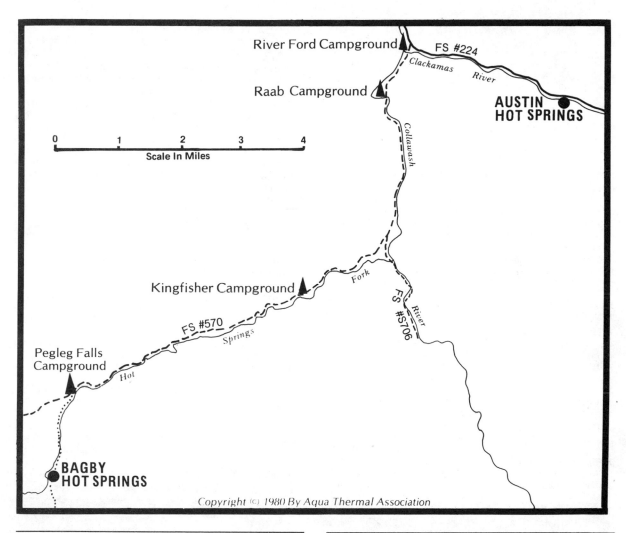

River Ford Campground   FS #224
Clackamas   River

Raab Campground

AUSTIN
HOT SPRINGS

Collawash

0   1   2   3   4
Scale In Miles

Kingfisher Campground

Fork

FS #S706

River

FS #570

Springs

Pegleg Falls
Campground

Hot

BAGBY
HOT SPRINGS

#174   BAGBY HOT SPRINGS   *(see map)*
*In Mt. Hood National Forest on the Hot Springs Fork of
the Collawash River.*

Status uncertain since bathhouse burned in 1979.
Primitive pools will be built by volunteers. The Forest
Service may rebuild some form of bathhouse. Elevation
2200 ft. Open all year.

Natural Mineral Water flows out the ground at more
than 120 degrees. Contact the Estacada Ranger Station
for information concerning pool rebuilding program, and
clothing policy, if any.

No facilities on the premises. 1½ miles to overnight
parking. 35 miles to all other services.

Source maps: Mt. Hood National Forest; USGS
-Battle Ax, Oregon.

#175   AUSTIN HOT SPRINGS   *(see map)*
In Mt. Hood National Forest on the Clackamas River.

A shady picnic ground (day use only) including several
hot springs which flow into dozens of primitive rock
pools along the edge of the stream. Elevation 1800 ft.
Open all year.

Natural Mineral Water flows out of the ground in
several places from 130 to 160 degrees, and cools in the
primitive pools on its way to the river. No clothing policy
is posted but suits are usually worn because the area is
popular and easily visible from the highway.

The grounds, including rest rooms, are owned and
maintained by the Portland Gas & Electric Company. 3
miles to a campground. 28 miles to all other services.

Source maps: Mt. Hood National Forest; USGS -Fish
Creek Mtn., Oregon.

#176 BOWMAN'S MOUNT HOOD RESORT
Welches   (503) 622-3101
Wemme, OR 97067   Therapy Pool   MH

#177 BAKER'S BAR M
Rte. 1   (503) 566-3381
Adams, OR 97810

Older guest ranch, with warm springs pool, surrounded by eastern Oregon prairie. Elevation 2200 ft. Open May through September.

Natural Mineral Water flows out of the ground at 90 degrees. Outdoor swimming pool (no chlorine) is maintained between 80 and 90 degrees. Bathing suits required.

Minimum stay, including meals and personal saddle horse, is one week, by advance reservation only. Pool available to registered guests only. No credit cards. 31 miles to all other services, including public bus.

From Interstate 80N, near Pendleton, take exit No. 216, turn left to blinking light, then right 1.5 miles, then left and follow signs approximately 22 miles to ranch.

#178 RITTER HOT SPRINGS
Box 16   (503) 421-3841
Ritter, OR 97872   PR + RV + MH

Historic old commercial resort with some buildings being modernized. Located in a rugged lava rock canyon in eastern Oregon. Elevation 2500 ft. Open all year.

Natural Mineral Water flows out of the ground at 109 degrees. Outdoor swimming pool (no chlorine) is maintained at 85 degrees and covered in winter. Four private indoor soaking pools are controllable to 109 degrees. Bathing suits required except in soaking pools.

Rooms, grocery store, gasoline and overnight parking spaces available on the premises. VISA and Mastercharge accepted. 17 miles to service station and full hook-up RV spaces. 61 miles to public bus.

From US 395, turn west on paved road along north bank of the John Day river, and follow signs to resort.

#179 COVE SWIMMING POOL
Rte. 1, Box 36   (503) 568-4890
Cove, OR 97824   PR

Rural community plunge and picnic grounds in the foothills of the Wallowa Mountains. Elevation 3200 ft. Open May 1 through Labor Day.

Natural Mineral Water flows out of the ground at 86 degrees, directly into outdoor swimming pool. No chlorine added. Bathing suits required.

Picnic grounds and overnight parking available on the premises. 8 miles to cafe, grocery store, service station, full hook-up RV spaces and tent spaces. 15 miles to motel and public bus.

On Oregon Route 237, 16 miles east of the town of La Grande.

#180 RADIUM HOT SPRINGS
Box 220   (503) 856-3609
Haines, OR 97833   PR + RV

Community plunge, picnic grounds and RV park, surrounded by the flat agricultural lands of Baker Valley. Elevation 3300 ft. Open June 1 through Labor Day.

Natural Mineral Water flows out of the ground at 135 degrees. Outdoor swimming pool is maintained at 90 to 95 degrees. Bathing suits required. Buildings are heated with geothermal energy.

Picnic grounds and overnight RV spaces available on the premises. No credit cards. 1 mile to cafe, grocery store and service station. 7 miles to motel. 12 miles to full hook-up RV spaces and public bus.

Located on US 30, 1 mile north of the town of Haines.

▶ RADIUM HOT SPRINGS: *Popular plunge.*

◣ SNIVELY HOT SPRING: *River's edge mix of hot and cold water in a rock pool.*

▼ RITTER HOT SPRINGS: *Historic stage stop which has become an all-year resort.*

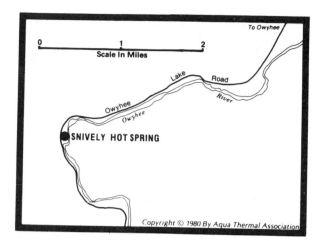

#181 SNIVELY HOT SPRING (see map)
30 miles south of the town of Ontario

Easily accessible primitive hot spring in the Owyhee River canyon 10 miles below Lake Owyhee. Elevation 2400 ft. Open all year.

Natural Mineral Water flows out of the ground at 120 + degrees in a small BLM picnic area on the bank of the Ohyhee River. Volunteers have built a primitive rock soaking pool at the edge of the stream, where mineral water and river water mix. The temperature is controllable by varying the amount of cold river water permitted to flow into the pool. There is no posted clothing policy, leaving it up to the mutual consent of those present.

The only service available on the premises is a picnic table and some room for overnight parking. 10 miles to cafe, service station and grocery store. 31 miles to all other services, including public bus.

Source map: USGS - Owyhee Dam, Oregon.

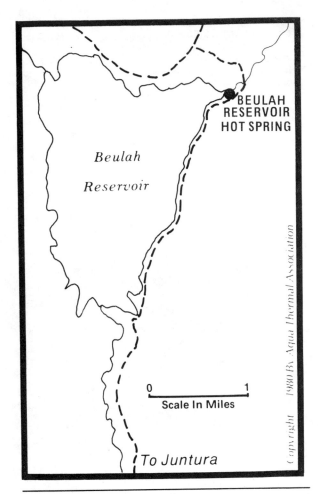

Beulah Reservoir

BEULAH
RESERVOIR
HOT SPRING

0   1
Scale In Miles

To Juntura

Copyright 1980 By Aqua Thermal Association

#183   ALVORD HOT SPRINGS   (see map)
On the western edge of the Alvord Desert in South-eastern Oregon.

Non-commercial semi-improved hot spring in the wide-open spaces at the foot of the Steens Mountains. Elevation 4000 ft. Open all year.

Natural Mineral Water flows out of the ground at 120 degrees, through a ditch to two cement soaking pools, one of them enclosed by sheets of galvanized steel. Temperature in each pool is controlled by diverting the 120 degree water as desired. There is no posted clothing policy, leaving it up to the mutual consent of those present.

No services available on the premises, but there is plenty of space along the gravel road for overnight parking. 25 miles to cafe and grocery store. 45 miles to all other services. 110 miles to public bus.

Source map: USGS - Alvord Hot Springs, Oregon.

#184   HART MOUNTAIN HOT SPRING   (see map)
In the Hart Mountain National Antelope Refuge, 35 miles north of the town of Adel.

Non-commercial semi-improved hot spring, enclosed by roofless cement block wall, and surrounded by miles of barren plateau. Elevation 6000 ft. Open all year.

Natural Mineral Water flows out of the ground at 98 degrees. The edge of the spring has been cemented to create a soaking pool which maintains that temperature. There is no posted clothing policy which leaves it up to the mutual consent of those present.

No services are available on the premises, but there is plenty of level space for overnight parking. 20 miles to grocery store and cafe. 40 miles to service station and motel. 75 miles to all other services, including public bus.

Source map: Hart Mountain National Antelope Refuge.

#182   BEULAH RESERVOIR HOT SPRING   (see map)
75 miles northeast of the town of Burns.

Remains of a one-tub bathhouse on Bureau of Land Management land in rugged foothills. Elevation 3300 ft. Open all year.

Natural Mineral Water flows out of the ground at more than 120 degrees, then flows through a long ditch to the reservoir. Along this ditch a local resident built a small bathhouse containing one enamel bathtub set in the concrete floor. The walls and roof have been totally vandalized, leaving only the tub and slab, plus a piece of garden hose to siphon water from the ditch to the tub. There is no posted clothing policy, leaving it up to the mutual consent of those present.

No services available on the premises. 1 mile to campground with tent spaces. 17 miles to motel, cafe, service station and grocery store. 75 miles to RV spaces and public bus.

Source map: USGS - Beulah, Oregon.

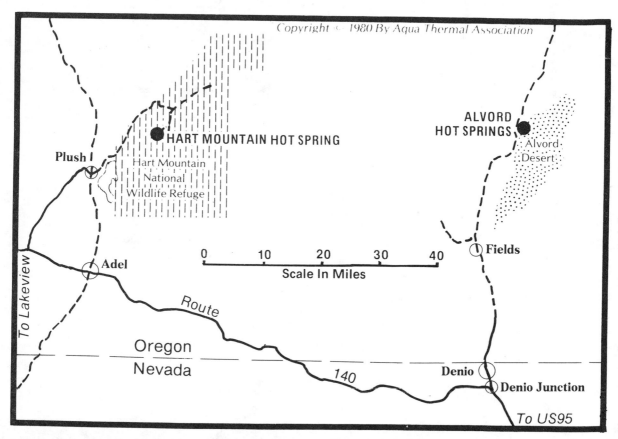

HART MOUNTAIN HOT SPRING

Plush

Hart Mountain
National
Wildlife Refuge

ALVORD
HOT SPRINGS

Alvord
Desert

0   10   20   30   40
Scale In Miles

Adel

To Lakeview

Route

Fields

Oregon

Nevada

140

Denio

Denio Junction

To US95

#185   HUNTER'S LODGE
Box 950
Lakeview, OR 97630

(503) 947-2127
MH

Motel, lounge and restaurant being expanded and remodeled. Elevation 4800 ft. Open all year.

Natural Mineral Water flows out of the ground at more than 180 degrees, in the form of Oregon's "Old Faithful Geyser". No swimming pools or soaking pools, but hot mineral water is piped to all motel bathrooms, and all buildings are geothermally heated. Long range expansion plans include soaking pools; telephone for information concerning construction progress.

Rooms, restaurant and camping spaces are available on the premises. VISA and Mastercharge accepted. 2 miles to all other services including public bus.

On US 395, two miles north of the town of Lakeview.

▲ *ALVORD HOT SPRINGS: The ultimate wide-open-spaces location for a hot spring. Popular with sand sailors from the desert.*

◀ *BEULAH RESERVOIR HOT SPRING: The end of the line for a remote bathhouse.*

43

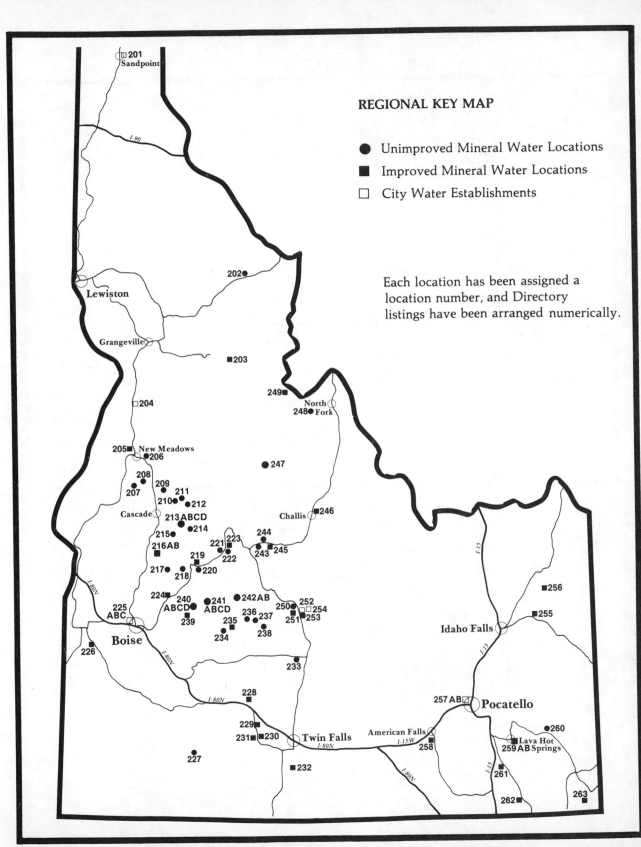

REGIONAL KEY MAP

● Unimproved Mineral Water Locations
■ Improved Mineral Water Locations
□ City Water Establishments

Each location has been assigned a location number, and Directory listings have been arranged numerically.

IDAHO:

Primitive Hot Pools Paradise

Basically, Idaho has two types of topography; the tree-clad mountainous slopes of the northern portion, and the partially irrigated arid plains along the Snake River in the south. All the hot springs in the easily accessible southern portion have been privately owned and commercially operated for many years. This is also true of the lower valleys in the northern portion. However, dozens of primitive geothermal flows are steaming and bubbling on National Forest property in the mountains of the north. Idaho has as many unimproved hot springs on publicly-owned land as all the other northwestern states put together.

A sizeable portion of the geothermal outflows occur on the banks, or in the walls, of canyons which have been carved out of the mountains by snow-fed rivers over the centuries. Also, during recent decades, some of these valleys have become routes for highways, logging roads or hiking trails. As a result, many of these primitive springs can be easily reached by highway, road or trail.

The South Fork of the Payette River, for example, is paralleled by Idaho Route 21, the main paved highway through the mountains to Montana. Of the half-dozen hot springs along this river, four are on National Forest property and the Forest Service has chosen to build full scale campgrounds adjoining two of them. A fifty yard stretch of riverside cliff

PINE FLATS HOT SPRINGS . . . . page 60

below Kirham Campground steams and trickles from a hundred openings, and the hot water cools as it cascades toward the river. Volunteers build and rebuild the many primitive rock pools to contain and further cool this mineral water to temperatures low enough for human tolerance. A soak in such a pool, with a rushing river below, trees across the river, and blue sky above, is the answer to a freeway driver's dream.

The Middle Fork of the Payette River has just as many hot springs but the Forest Service gravel road stops at Boiling Springs Guard Station. A hiking trail goes on upstream, fording the river when necessary, to reach several more undeveloped geothermal flows.

The Middle Fork of the Salmon River is equally blessed with hot mineral water, but having been designated a Wilderness Area, it has no roads or motor vehicles of any kind. These remote springs can only be reached by floating down river on a raft, and then eventually floating on to the main Salmon River, where a gravel road leads one back to civilization.

Nearly all of Idaho's mountain hot springs spew from the ground at more than 115 degrees, so some form of cooling is necessary before a soak is possible. This is usually accomplished by building a primitive rock pool at the point where the hot water runs into the nearby creek or river, so that the temperature can be adjusted by controlling the amount of cold river water added to the geothermal water. Such an arrangement also provides the thrill of stepping directly into the melted snow river water if change from the hot water is desired.

In one sense, the phrase "primitive hot pool" is also appropriate for some of the older developed resorts, where, for years, the mineral water has simply flowed through a cedar or plaster-lined pool, without gutters, filters, chlorinators or life guards. In recent years the Regional (County) Health Departments have been closing down such pools, applying present-day Idaho standards for building city swimming pools containing gas-heated city water. Believe it or not, these state standards do not contain provisions for the unique problems and potentials of hot mineral water, and the Idaho Health Department has no plans to create such standards.

In addition to all its mineral water pools, Idaho also has the distinction of hosting one of the first rent-a-tub establishments in the Northwest. Apparently, the magic of hot spring mineral water is nowadays less important than the convenience of being able to rent a private patio containing a hot pool

WARM SPRINGS CAMPGROUND . . . . page 62

46

right in the middle of town. THE HOT SPOT, in Ketchum, does a thriving business with its gas-heated city water hot tubs, even though there are dozens of natural hot mineral springs within 100 miles.

Geothermal Energy

A few of the older hot springs resorts, such as Twin Springs, Miracle Springs and Banbury Hot Springs, have been using geothermal space heating in their buildings for years. Withing the last two decades geothermal heating of greenhouses has been initiated at Green Canyon, Warm Springs and White Arrow. The location of White Arrow is ideal for distilling methanol from agricultural waste, and the owner is actively working toward contracting for a demonstration project.

The American Potato Company and Madison County are working together on a two-stage DOE-funded demonstration project. It is designed to supply hot mineral water to heat exchangers for industrial processing use at the potato company, after which the partially-cooled mineral water will be cascaded on to county heat exchangers to provide space and water heating in nearby county buildings.

In the eastern part of Boise, district geothermal heating of homes and buildings has been going on for nearly a century. A local Water District operates the wells and distribution pipes, which are now also being connected to newly-constructed condominiums. This Water District and the city of Boise have joined in a major DOE-funded demonstration project designed to refurbish the existing facilities, drill new wells and install new distribution pipes to downtown Boise to supply federal, state and county buildings. A shopping mall, and other commercial buildings are also included in the long range plans.

Preliminary studies for district heating have also been started on the towns of Hailey, Ketchum and Fairfield, each of which has a proven geothermal resource nearby.

The following codes were used in the preparation of listings and maps on the following pages.

NATURAL MINERAL WATER LOCATIONS ARE SET IN BOLD TYPE — like this
GAS HEATED CITY WATER LOCATIONS ARE SET IN REGULAR TYPE — like this

PR = Tubs or pools for rent, by hour, day or treatment.
MH = Rooms or cabins for rent by day, week or month.
RV = Vehicle spaces for rent by day, week, month, or year.

Open all year means that there are no doors or gates closed during a part of the year. However, snow or high water may temporarily make the location inaccessible.

——————— Paved highway
– — – — Gravel or dirt road
·············· Hiking trail
▲ Campground

48

JERRY JOHNSON'S HOT SPRINGS:
Mineral water spurts from dozens of places at a temperature too hot to touch.

Each rock pool has a different combination of cold creek water and hot spring water.

#201 EDGEWATER LODGE
Box 128
Sandpoint, ID 83864

(208) 263-3194
Hydrojet Pool MH

#202 JERRY JOHNSON'S HOT SPRING   (see map)
On the Lewis and Clark Highway in Clearwater National Forest.

Several unimproved hot springs along a ¼ mile of Warm Springs Creek, reached by a 1 mile pack trail. Elevation 4000 ft. Open all year.

Natural Mineral Water flows out of the ground at temperatures up to 120 degrees. Volunteers have built many primitive rock and log pools near the springs and along the edge of the stream, providing a wide variety of soaking temperatures. There is no posted clothing policy, which leaves it up to the mutual consent of those present.

No services available on the premises. Two miles to Forest Service Campground. 30 miles to all other services.

Source maps: Clearwater National Forest; USGS -Bear Mountain and Tom Beal Peak, Idaho.

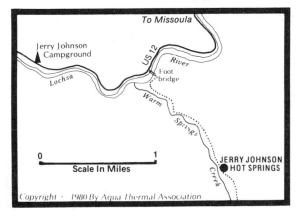

#203 RED RIVER HOT SPRINGS

(208) 983-0452

Elk City, ID 83525

PR + MH

Historic rustic resort on edge of Selway-Bitterroot Wilderness, in scenic National Forest cul-de-sac. Elevation 4500 ft. Open all year - by sno-cat only from December to April.

Natural Mineral Water flows out of the ground at 138 degrees. Outdoor swimming pool - 72 degrees in winter to 97 degrees in summer. Four indoor soaking pools in private rooms, controllable to 110 degrees. Bathing suits required except in private rooms.

Rooms and restaurant available on the premises. No credit cards. 25 miles to all other services. 75 miles to public bus.

From the town of Grangeville, take Idaho Route 14 to Elk City, then 25 miles south and east to resort. Gravel road for last 11 miles.

49

#204   SQUAW CREEK CAMPGROUND
Box 438   (208) 628-3455
Riggins, ID 83459   PR + RV + MH

Teepee Motel and campground with hot pool. Elevation 1800 ft. Open May through October.

Gas-heated city water in fiberglass hydrojet tub. 100 degrees. Bathing suits required.

Picnic area, teepees and full hook-up RV spaces available on the premises. VISA and Mastercharge accepted. 1 mile to all other services, including public bus.

Located on US 95, 1 mile south of the town of Riggins.

#205   ZIM'S HOT SPRINGS
Box 314   (208) 347-2115
New Meadows, ID 83654   PR + RV

Rural plunge, picnic grounds and campground in agricultural valley surrounded by National Forest. Elevation 4200 ft. Open all year.

Natural Mineral Water flows out of the ground at 151 degrees. Outdoor swimming pool - 90 to 100 degrees. Outdoor soaking pool (no chlorine) 103 to 106 degrees. Bathing suits required.

Restaurant, picnic area and overnight RV spaces available on the premises. No credit cards. 4 miles to all other services, including public bus.

From the town of New Meadow, take US 95 4 miles north, then follow signs to resort.

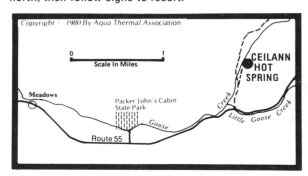

#206   CEILANN HOT SPRING   (see map)
Near the town of Meadows.

Unimproved hot spring on east bank of Goose Creek in timbered portion of Payette National Forest. Elevation 400 ft. Open all year.

Natural Mineral Water flows out of the ground at 102 degrees, and is piped to primitive rock pool built by volunteers. 85 to 95 degrees, depending on wind and air temperature. There is no posted clothing policy, which leaves it up to the mutual consent of those present.

No services available on the premises. 2 miles to picnic area, grocery store and service station. 9 miles to all other services, including public bus.

Source maps: Payette National Forest; Meadows, Idaho.

50

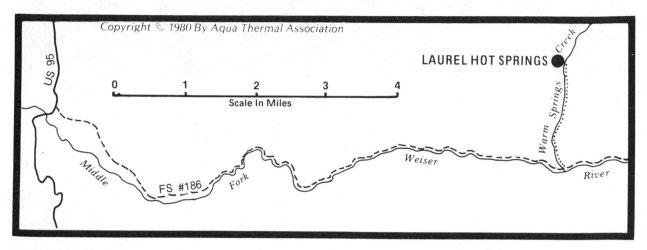

LAUREL HOT SPRINGS

US 95

0   1   2   3   4
Scale In Miles

Middle   FS #186   Fork

Weiser

Warm Springs Creek

River

▼ ZIM'S HOT SPRINGS: *The air spray method cools water going into the pool.*

◄ CEILANN HOT SPRING: *Running part of the spring water through a pipe provides a stand-up shower as well as a soaking pool.*

▼ LAUREL HOT SPRINGS: *Soaking will be possible after the rock dam is rebuilt.*

#207   LAUREL HOT SPRINGS   *(see map)*
Near the town of Council.

Several unimproved thermal springs in a steep wooded canyon at the end of a rugged 1 mile trail in Payette National Forest. Elevation 4300 ft. Open all year.

Natural Mineral Water flows out of the ground at more than 120 degrees, into a primitive rock pool on the bank of Warm Springs Creek. Temperature controllable by allowing more or less cold creek water into pool. The local custom is clothing optional.

No services available on the premises. 7 miles to picnic area and campground. 23 miles to all other services. 38 miles to public bus.

Source maps: Payette National Forest; USGS ·Council, Idaho.

#208 WHITE LICKS HOT SPRING (see map)
Near the town of Donnelly.

Several springs serving two small bathhouses in a wooded campground in the Payette National Forest. Elevation 4800 ft. Open all year.

Natural Mineral Water flows out of several springs at temperatures up to 120 degrees, supplying two small wood shacks, each containing a cement tub. Each tub is served by two plastic pipes, one bringing 110 + degree water; the other bringing 80 degree water. Tub temperature is controlled by plugging up the pipe bringing the temperature not desired. Soakers are expected to drain the tub after each use. Bathing suits not required inside bathhouses.

Picnic area and campground available on the premises. 16 miles to all other services. 30 miles to public bus.

Source map: Payette National Forest; USGS ·Cascade, Idaho.

#209 GOLD FORK HOT SPRING (see map)
Near the town of Donnelly.

Non-commercial primitive hot spring in wooded foothills on the edge of Boise National Forest. Elevation 5200 ft. Open all year.

Natural Mineral Water flows out of the ground at a temperature of more than 120 degrees, and gradually cools in a series of substantial log pools built by volunteers. Upper pool · 107 to 110 degrees. Second pool · 105 degrees. A porcelain bathtub is set to receive the small waterfall overflow from second pool. Third pool ·95 degrees. There is no posted clothing policy, which leaves it up to the mutual consent of those present.

Space for picnics and parking is available near the spring. 6 miles to motel, restaurant, service station and grocery store. 16 miles to full hook-up RV spaces. 90 miles to public bus.

Source maps: Boise National Forest; USGS · Gold Fork, Idaho.

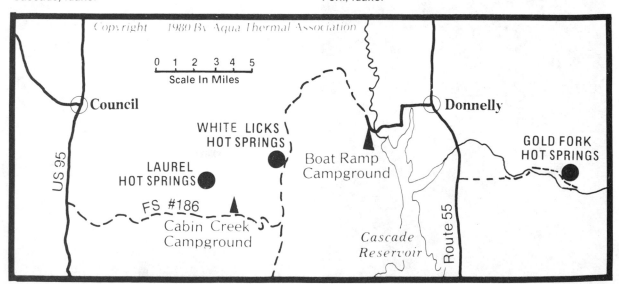

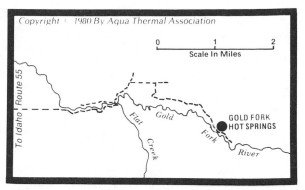

0   1   2
Scale In Miles

To Idaho Route 55

Gold Fork

Flat Creek

GOLD FORK
HOT SPRINGS

River

▲ GOLD FORK HOT SPRING: The last pool in the series has the coolest water.

◀ A splash spray helps cool the upper pool.

▼ A porcelain bathtub receives the run-off from the therapy-temperature middle pool.

53

#210　BREIT (TRAIL CREEK) HOT SPRING　(see map)
Near the town of Cascade.

Unimproved hot spring on side of steep canyon in Boise National Forest. Elevation 6000 ft. Open all year.

Natural Mineral Water flows out of a fissure in the rocks at more than 115 degrees. Volunteers have built a primitive rock pool on the edge of Trail Creek, where the hot and cold water can be mixed by controlling the amount of cold creek water admitted. There is no posted clothing policy, which leaves it up to the mutual consent of those present.

No services available at the spring, which is a steep 200 ft. climb down from the roadside parking area. 3 miles to campground. 22 miles to all other services, including public bus.

Source maps: Boise National Forest.

#211　MOLLY'S HOT SPRING　(see map)
Near the town of Cascade.

Unimproved hot spring on steep slope in timbered portion of Boise National Forest. Elevation 5400 ft. Open all year.

Natural Mineral Water flows out of several springs at more than 120 degrees, then down the slope to South Fork of the Salmon River. Some pipes are still in place from the time when this was the source spring for the Warm Lake Plunge, now closed. Volunteers have built a small primitive rock pool to collect partially cooled water for soaking. Pool temperature depends on wind and air temperature. The local custom is clothing optional.

No services available on the premises. 2 miles to campground. 25 miles to all other services, including public bus.

Source maps: Boise National Forest.

#212　VULCAN HOT SPRINGS　(see map)
Near the town of Cascade.

Large geothermal area in a timbered portion of Boise National Forest. Elevation 5600 ft. Open all year.

Natural Mineral Water flows out of many bubbling springs at boiling temperature, creating a substantial hot creek, which gradually cools as it runs through the woods toward the South Fork of the Salmon River. Volunteers have built a log dam across this creek at the point where the water has cooled to approximately 105 degrees. There is no posted clothing policy, which leaves it up to the mutual consent of those present.

No services available at the springs, reached by a ½ mile trail from an unofficial camping area. 10 miles to campground. 32 miles to all other services, including public bus.

Source maps: Boise National Forest; USGS - Warm Lake, Idaho.

▲ *BREIT HOT SPRING:　A creek-bottom pool as seen from parking area off paved highway.*

► *VULCAN HOT SPRINGS:　The entire flow of the creek comes from boiling springs a quarter mile upstream from this log dam.*

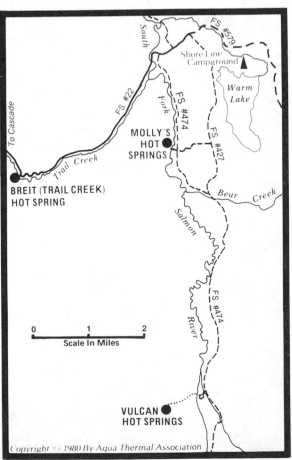

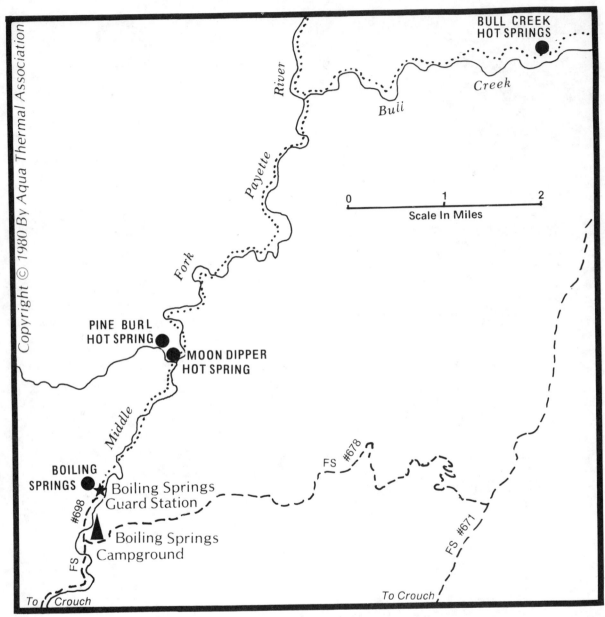

BULL CREEK
HOT SPRINGS

River

Creek

Bull

Payette

Scale In Miles
0   1   2

Fork

PINE BURL
HOT SPRING

MOON DIPPER
HOT SPRING

Middle

FS #678

BOILING
SPRINGS

Boiling Springs
Guard Station

#698

FS

Boiling Springs
Campground

FS #671

To Crouch

To Crouch

#213A   BULL CREEK HOT SPRINGS   *(see map)*
Near the town of Crouch.

Unimproved hot spring on the bank of Bull Creek, in Boise National Forest. Elevation 4600 ft. Open all year.

Natural Mineral Water flows out of the ground at more than 120 degrees, into primitive rock pools along the edge of the creek. Pool temperature controlled by admit-ting more or less cold creek water. The local custom is clothing optional.

No services available on the premises. 9 miles to campground. 29 miles to all other services. 78 miles to public bus.

Source maps: Boise National Forest; USGS -Boiling Springs, Idaho.

#213B   MOON DIPPER HOT SPRING   (see map)
Near the town of Crouch.

Unimproved hot spring on the bank of Dash Creek, in the Boise National Forest. Elevation 4200 ft. Open all year.

Natural Mineral Water flows out of the bank at 120 degrees. Volunteers have built a primitive rock pool where the mineral water and creek water are mixed to the desired temperature. The local custom is clothing optional.

No services available on the premises. 1½ miles by trail to campground. 21 miles to all other services. 70 miles to public bus.

Source maps: Boise National Forest; USGS · Boiling Springs, Idaho.

#213C   PINE BURL HOT SPRING   (see map)
Near the town of Crouch.

Unimproved hot spring on the bank of Dash Creek in Boise National Forest. Elevation 4200 ft. Open all year.

Natural Mineral Water flows out of the ground at 120 degrees, directly into primitive rock pool built by volunteers. Water temperature in the pool is varied by controlling the amount of cold creek water admitted through a pipe. The local custom is clothing optional.

No services available on the premises. 1½ miles by trail to campground. 21 miles to all other services. 70 miles to public bus.

Source maps: Boise National Forest: USGS · Boiling Springs, Idaho.

#213D   BOILING SPRINGS   (see map)
Near the town of Crouch.

Large geothermal water flow on the Middle Fork of the Payette River in Boise National Forest. Elevation 4200 ft. Open all year.

Natural Mineral Water flows out of a cliff at more than 130 degrees, into a pond adjoining the Boiling Springs Guard Station. The water cools as it flows through a ditch to join the river. Some summer volunteers dam up the ditch at the point where the water is cool enough for soaking. There are no posted clothing requirements, which leaves it up to the mutual consent of those present.

Campground available on the premises. 19 miles to all other services. 68 miles to public bus.

Source maps: Boise National Forest; USGS · Boiling Springs, Idaho.

▶ *MOON DIPPER HOT SPRING: Ingenious inflow channels permit adding hot or cold water to this pool whenever needed.*

◀ *Names for such remote springs are chosen by the volunteers who build the pools.*

57

▲ SILVER CREEK PLUNGE: *A swim pool athlete attempts an inner tube long jump.*

▼ ROBERTS HOT SPRING: *This hillside pool has a plastic liner to hold the water in.*

#214 SILVER CREEK PLUNGE

(208) 344-8688 (ask for unit 1270)

Garden Valley, ID 83622   PR + RV + MH

Rural mountain resort surrounded by Boise National Forest. Elevation 4600 ft. Open May through November.

Natural Mineral Water flows out of the ground at 101 degrees. Outdoor swimming pool · 84 degrees. Bathing suits required.

Cabins, picnic area and campsites available on the premises. No credit cards. 23 miles to all other services. 75 miles to public bus. ⁓

From the town of Crouch, take the Middle Fork road for 14 miles, then follow signs east 9 miles to plunge.

#215 ROBERTS HOT SPRING (see map)
Near the town of Crouch.

Unimproved hot spring in Boise National Forest. Elevation 4000 ft. Open all year.

Natural Mineral Water flows out of the ground at 120 degrees, then down a steep slope toward Middle Fork of Payette River. To reach the spring the river must be waded, which might not be safe during high water. Volunteers have built a series of primitive rock pools, each cooler than the one above. The local custom is clothing optional.

No services available on the premises. ½ mile to picnic area. 1 mile to campground. 10 miles to all other services. 65 miles to public bus.

Source maps: Boise National Forest.

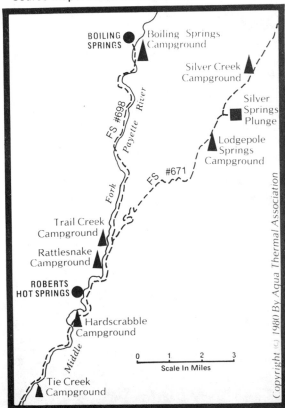

▲ *TERRACE LAKES RECREATIONAL RANCH:*
Country club atmosphere at forest's edge.

▶ *WARM SPRINGS GREENHOUSE: Hot*
water is run through this overhead radiator
to keep the thousands of flowers warm.

#216A   TERRACE LAKES RECREATIONAL RANCH
Garden Valley, ID 83622   *(208) 462-3250*

Private membership recreation ranch in rolling foothills. Elevation 3300 ft. Open all year.

Natural Mineral Water flows out of the ground at 176
degrees. Outdoor swimming pool - 90 to 100 degrees.
Bathing suits required.

Golf, restaurant, tennis and full hook-up RV spaces
available on the premises; for the exclusive use of
members and their guests. 4 miles to grocery store and
service station. 13 miles to public bus. 18 miles to campground. 50 miles to motel.

From the town of Crouch, go three miles north on the
Middle Fork Road, then follow signs 1 mile to resort.

#216B   WARM SPRINGS GREENHOUSE
Star Route   *(208) 462-3225*
Garden Valley, ID 83622

Large (40,000 sq. ft.) geothermal nursery. Elevation
3400 ft. Visitors welcome by prior arrangement.

Natural Mineral Water flows out of the ground at 176
degrees, supplying heat for an acre of greenhouses, full
of cut flowers and azaleas. No facilities for personal
soaking.

No services available on the premises. Phone for permission to visit, and directions to the location.

59

#217 HOT SPRINGS CAMPGROUND
Near the town of Crouch.

National Forest Campground on the South Fork of the Payette River in the Boise National Forest. Elevation 3800 ft. Open all year.

Natural Mineral Water flows out of the ground at 105 degrees, supplying several primitive rock pools built by volunteers along the edge of the river. Only cement foundations remain of bathhouses which were dismantled several years ago. Bathing suits advisable, at least during daylight hours.

Picnic area and camping sites are available in the upper portion of the campground (north of the highway). 5 miles to all other services. 65 miles to public bus.

From the town of Banks, on Idaho Route 55, go north to Crouch intersection, then east through Crouch and Garden Valley, on the road to Lowman.

#218 PINE FLATS HOT SPRINGS
Near the town of Lowman.

National Forest Campground adjoining thermal area on the South Fork of the Payette River. Elevation 4100 ft. Open all year.

Natural Mineral Water flows out of the side of the canyon more than 50 ft. above the river, at more than 120 degrees, cooling as it cascades over the rocks. One primitive rock pool has been built by volunteers part way up the bank; others have been built along the edge of the river. Temperatures vary with wind, air temperature and proportion of river water. Bathing suits advisable at least during daylight hours.

Campground and picnic area available on the premises. 4 miles to motel, restaurant, grocery store and service station. 35 miles to full hook-up RV spaces.

Located on gravel road connecting Lowman and Crouch, 4 miles west of Lowman.

#219 HAVEN LODGE
General Delivery   (no phone)
Lowman, ID 83637   PR + RV + MH

Motel and RV park with pools and tubs along South Fork of Payette River. Elevation 4000 ft. Open all year.

Natural Mineral Water flows out of the ground at 148 degrees. Outdoor swimming pool · 80 to 90 degrees. Two indoor individual tubs in private rooms · controllable temperatures. Bathing suits required except in private rooms.

Cabins, restaurant, service station, full hook-up RV spaces and picnic area available on the premises. 4 miles to grocery store. 78 miles to public bus.

Located on Idaho Route 21, 3 ½ miles east of the town of Lowman.

▶ *PINE FLATS HOT SPRINGS: This pool is built 30 ft. up the cliff toward the source springs, which are another 50 ft. farther up the face of crumbling rocks.*

KIRKHAM HOT SPRINGS: This popular site is served by a highway and a campground.

High visibility makes clothing a necessity, which creates some problems while showering.

#220 KIRKHAM HOT SPRINGS
Near the town of Lowman.

National Forest Campground adjoining large thermal area on the South Fork of the Payette River. Elevation 4200 ft. Open all year.

Natural Mineral Water flows out of many springs along a ¼ mile of riverbank, at temperatures up to 120 degrees, into dozens of primitive rock pools constructed by volunteers. Also 4 indoor individual tubs with controllable temperatures. Bathing suits advisable at least during daylight hours.

Campground and picnic area available on the premises. 2 miles to motel, restaurant, grocery store and service station. 34 miles to full hook-up RV spaces.

Located on Idaho Route 21, 4 miles east of the town of Lowman.

#221 WARM SPRINGS CAMPGROUND
Near the town of Lowman.

National Forest campground adjoining large thermal area in Boise National Forest. Elevation 4800 ft. Open all year.

Natural Mineral Water flows out of many springs over a space of several acres, with various temperatures up to 170 degrees. Volunteers have built many primitive rock pools at the edge of Warm Springs Creek, providing a variety of soaking temperatures. Also one small bath-house with an individual tub, supplied by a nearby spring at 103 degrees. Bathing suits advisable except in bathhouse.

Picnic area and campsites available in the lower section of the campground, ¼ mile away by trail. 14 miles to all other services. 48 miles to full hook-up RV spaces and public bus.

Located 18 miles east of Lowman on Idaho Route 21.

#222 SACAJAWEA HOT SPRINGS
Near the town of Lowman.

Large geothermal area on the north bank of the South Fork of the Payette River, in the Boise National Forest.

Natural Mineral Water flows out of many springs at temperatures up to 180 degrees, into a series of primitive rock pools built by volunteers along the edge of the water. Bathing suits are advisable, at least during the daylight hours.

No services available on the premises. 1 mile to cabins, restaurants, and full hook-up RV spaces. 28 miles to grocery store and service station. 61 miles to public bus.

From the town of Lowman, on Idaho Route 21, go 22 miles east, then follow signs toward Sawtooth Lodge on gravel road for 5 miles. Springs and pools extend along the south side of the road.

#223 SAWTOOTH LODGE
Boise phone #(208) 344-6685
Grandjean, ID 83637   *RV + MH*

Historic mountain resort in the Sawtooth Recreation Area. Elevation 5100 ft. Open June through October.

Natural Mineral water flows out of the ground at 100 degrees. Outdoor swimming pool - 80 degrees. Bathing suits required.

Cabins, restaurant and full hook-up RV spaces available on the premises. Visa and Mastercharge accepted. 28 miles to grocery store and service station. 62 miles to public bus.

From the town of Lowman, on Idaho Route 21, go 22 miles east, then follow signs 6 miles on gravel road to lodge.

◀ *WARM SPRINGS CAMPGROUND: There are many soaking pools in this geothermal area, a short hike from a complete Forest Service campground just off a main highway.*

 SACAJAWEA HOT SPRINGS: Another roadside outflow feeds riverside rock pools.

▶ WARM SPRINGS RESORT: Historic site with plans for further modernization.

#224   WARM SPRINGS RESORT
Box 28   (208) 392-4437
Idaho City, ID 83631   PR + RV + MH

Rural plunge and RV park surrounded by Boise National Forest. Elevation 4000 ft. Open all year, but limited to weekends and holidays during the winter.

Natural Mineral Water flows out of the ground at 110 degrees. Outdoor pool (R&R music) - 94 to 98 degrees. Bathing suits required.

Cabins, picnic area and full hook-up RV spaces available on the premises. 2 miles to other services. 35 miles to public bus.

Located on State Route 21, 1½ miles south of the town of Idaho City.

#225A   INTERNATIONAL DUNES MOTEL
3031 Main St.   (208) 344-3521
Boise, ID 83706   Therapy Pool   MH

#225B   HOLIDAY INN
3300 Vista Ave.   (208) 344-8365
Boise, ID 83705   Hydrojet Pool   MH

#225C   ROYAL INN
1115 N. Curtis Rd.   (208) 376-2700
Boise, ID 83704   Hydrojet Pool   MH

63

▲ *GIVENS HOT SPRINGS: Private pool room and adjoining main swimming pool.*

▼ *INDIAN BATHTUB: Picturesque setting for a rapidly dwindling geothermal flow.*

#226   GIVENS HOT SPRINGS
Star Route   **(208) 495-2437**
Melba, ID 83641   **PR**
   Rural plunge and picnic park on agricultural plateau above the Snake River. Elevation 3000 ft. Open all year.
   Natural Mineral Water flows out of the ground at 120 to 130 degrees. Indoor swimming pool - 100 degrees. Six indoor soaking pools in private rooms - controllable temperature. Bathing suits required except in private rooms. Tent spaces and picnic grounds available on the premises. 11 miles to all other services, including public bus.
   Located 11 miles southeast of the town of Marsing on Idaho Route 78.

#227   INDIAN BATHTUB   *(see map)*
Near the town of Bruneau.
   Unimproved soaking pool in rugged cliffs on Bureau of Land Management property. Access is over very rough roads and down a steep cliff. Elevation 2400 ft. Open all year.
   Natural Mineral Water flows out of rock formation at 93 degrees, into canyon bottom, where centuries of erosion have scoured out shallow pockets in the rock. Volunteers have added a primitive rock dam to deepen the main sandy-bottom soaking pool, which maintains a temperature of 85 to 91 degrees. There is no posted clothing policy, which leaves it up to the mutual consent of those present. Examination of past records shows that the volume of hot water flow has been decreased dramatically due to nearby irrigation pumping since the days when local Indian tribes prized this mineral water oasis in an otherwise arid land.
   No services available on the premises except a small amount of level parking area at the top of the cliff. 11 miles to grocery store and service station. 26 miles to all other services, including public bus.
   Source maps: USGS - Hot Spring and Sugar Valley, Idaho.

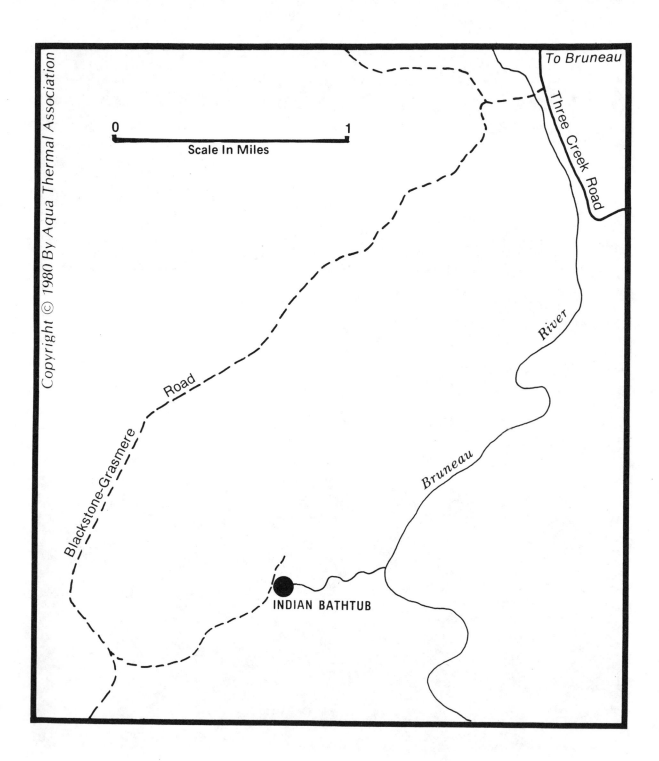

To Bruneau

Three Creek Road

River

Bruneau

0   1
Scale In Miles

Blackstone-Grasmere   Road

INDIAN BATHTUB

#228   WHITE ARROW
Box 108
Bliss, ID 83314

Greenhouse and fish hatchery which was formerly a major Indian campground and stagecoach stop. Elevation 3400 ft. Visitors welcome by prior arrangement.

Natural Mineral Water flows out of the ground at 151 degrees. Geothermal heat is used in greenhouses, fish ponds, residence, personal swimming pool and walkways exposed to snow. Plans are in process to use agricultural waste in an alcohol distillation plant operated on geothermal heat.

No public facilities available on the premises. Use correspondence to arrange for visit and obtain directions.

#229   SLIGAR'S THOUSAND SPRINGS RESORT
Rte. 1, Box 90   *(208) 837-4987*
Hagerman, ID 83332   *PR + RV*

Rural plunge, rental tubs and RV park on the south bank of the Snake River. Elevation 2900 ft. Open all year.

Natural Mineral Water flows out of the ground at 200 degrees. Outdoor swimming pool · 90 to 96 degrees. 17 indoor private soaking and jet pools · controllable temperatures. Bathing suits required except in private rooms.

Full hook-up RV spaces, picnic area, fishing and boat dock available on the premises. ¼ mile to all other services. 5 miles to public bus.

Located on US 30, 5 miles south of the town of Hagerman.

◀ *SLIGAR'S THOUSAND SPRING RESORT: Several new private pools are being built.*

▼ *A large log in the indoor swim pool tests the balance of young acrobatic swimmers.*

▲ BANBURY HOT SPRINGS: *This outdoor swim pool offers a balancing log similar to the one at Sligar's.*

▶ *Banbury's electric power is generated here by the flow of hot mineral water through pipes from springs in the cliffs on the other side of the Snake River.*

▼ *Campgrounds occupy several acres along the river.*

#230 BANBURY HOT SPRINGS
Rte. 3   *(208) 543-4098*
Buhl, ID 83316   *PR + RV*

Plunge, RV park and picnic grounds, on south bank of Snake River. Elevation 3000 ft. Open all year, except swimming pool open from May to Labor Day.

Natural Mineral Water flows out of the ground at 131 degrees. Outdoor swimming pool · 89 to 95 degrees. Two indoor individual tubs with hydromassage units · controllable temperatures. Bathing suits required except in private rooms. Geothermal heat in all locker rooms and buildings. Inflow of hot water also used to generate electricity used on the grounds.

Full hook-up RV spaces, spacious tree-shaded picnic grounds, boat ramp and boat rental available on the premises. No credit cards. 12 miles to all other services, including public bus.

Located on US 30, 12 miles west of the town of Buhl.

MIRACLE HOT SPRINGS: This pool offers an overwater trapeze bar.

Each of the roofless private pools has its own hot water inlet control valve.

#231 MIRACLE HOT SPRINGS
Box 171   (208) 543-4740
Buhl, ID 83316   PR + RV

Older health spa surrounded by rolling agricultural land. Elevation 3000 ft. Open all year.

Natural Mineral Water is pumped out of the ground at 139 degrees. Outdoor swimming pool - 95 degrees. Outdoor soaking pool - 100 + degrees. 15 roofless enclosed soaking pools - controllable temperatures. No chlorine in any pools. Bathing suits required except in enclosed pools. All buildings and dressing rooms supplied with geothermal heat.

Overnight RV spaces and picnic area available on the premises. 12 miles to all other services, including public bus.

Located on US 30, 10 miles northwest of the town of Buhl.

#232 NAT SOO PAH HOT SPRING
Rte 1   (208) 655-9925
Twin Falls, ID 83301   PR + RV

Rural swimming pool and camp ground. Elevation 5000 ft. Open May to Labor Day.

Natural Mineral Water flows out of the ground at 98 degrees. Outdoor swimming pool - 80 to 84 degrees. Bathing suits required.

Picnic area and overnite RV spaces available on the premises. No credit cards. 3 miles to restaurant, grocery store and service station. 16 miles to motel, full hook-up RV spaces and public bus.

From Twin Falls go 16 miles south on South Blue Lake Road. Follow signs to resort.

#233 HOT SPRINGS LANDING (see map)
AT MAGIC RESERVOIR
Near the town of Bellevue in rolling foothills south of the Sawtooth National Forest.

Abandoned hot spring and small boat landing on the edge of near-empty reservoir. Elevation 5100 ft. Open all year.

Natural Mineral Water flows out of the ground at over 170 degrees. A hose takes a portion of the output to an unattended wooden hot tub overlooking the reservoir. Temperature of water in tub can be controlled by removing hot water supply hose. Bathing suits advisable at least in daylight hours.

No services available on the premises. 15 miles to all services.

Source map: USGS - Bellvue, Idaho.

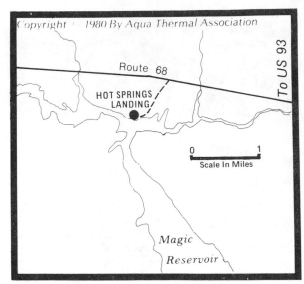

HOT SPRINGS LANDING AT MAGIC RESERVOIR: This wood tub sits just above the waterline when the reservoir is full. By late summer storage reaches a minimum.

#234 AURORA HOT SPRINGS (see map)
Near the town of Featherville in Sawtooth National Forest.

Unimproved hot spring on the east bank of the South Fork of the Boise River. Elevation 4400 ft. Open all year.

Natural Mineral Water flows out of the ground at 128 degrees, supplying several primitive rock pools built by volunteers along the edge of the river. All pools are clearly visible from the highway, so bathing suits are advisable.

No services on the premises. 1 mile to campground. 6 miles to rooms, restaurant, service station and grocery store. 39 miles to full hook-up RV spaces and public bus.

Source map: Sawtooth National Forest.

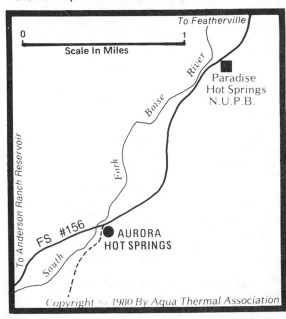

▲ *BAUMGARTNER HOT SPRINGS:* The Forest Service pays a local crew to clean the pool weekly.

#235   *BAUMGARTNER HOT SPRINGS*   (see map)
Near the town of Featherville, in Sawtooth National Forest.

Well-maintained cement soaking pool in a National Forest Campground. Elevation 5000 ft. Open all year.

Natural Mineral Water flows out of the ground at 105 degrees, supplying the soaking pool on a flow-through (no chlorine) basis, which maintains the pool temperature at 104 degrees. Because of location in a campground, bathing suits are advisable, at least during daylight hours.

Campground facilities available on the premises. 11 miles to rooms, restaurant, service station and grocery store. 48 miles to full hook-up RV spaces and public bus.

Source maps: Sawtooth National Forest: USGS - Jumbo Mtn., Idaho.

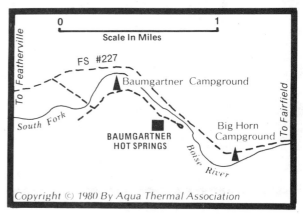

0   1
Scale In Miles

To Featherville

FS #227

Baumgartner Campground

To Fairfield

South Fork

BAUMGARTNER HOT SPRINGS

Big Horn Campground

Boise River

#236   SKILLERN HOT SPRINGS   (see map)
Near the town of Featherville in Sawtooth National Forest.

Unimproved hot spring on Big Smokey Creek, 3 miles by trail from Paradise Creek Campground. Trail fords stream several times, and might not be passable during high water season. Elevation 5800 ft. Open all year.

Natural Mineral Water flows out of the ground at more than 110 degrees, supplying a primitive rock pool built by volunteers at the edge of Big Smokey Creek. Pool temperature is controllable by varying the amount of cold creek water admitted. The local custom is clothing optional.

No services on the premises. 3 miles to campground. 24 miles to all other services. 81 miles to public bus.

Source maps: Sawtooth National Forest; USGS ·Sydney Butte and Paradise Peak, Idaho.

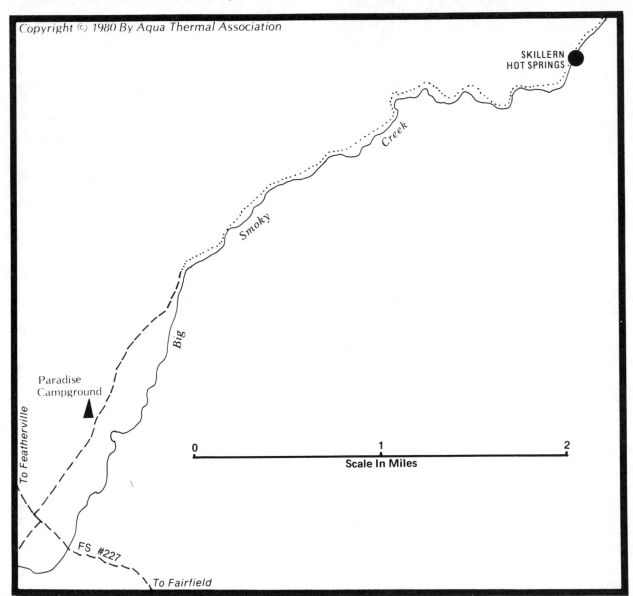

SKILLERN HOT SPRINGS

Creek

Smoky

Big

Paradise Campground

To Featherville

FS #227

To Fairfield

0   1   2
Scale In Miles

PREIS HOT SPRING: *This is definitely the smallest improved hot spring pool anywhere.*

WORSWICK HOT SPRINGS: *The hot water keeps flowing, with or without a resort.*

#237   PREIS HOT SPRING   (see map)
Near the town of Fairfield in Sawtooth National Forest.

Small 1-person soaking pit by the side of the road. Elevation 6000 ft. Open all year.

Natural Mineral Water flows out of the ground at 94 degrees, directly into small pool which has been given board sides large enough to accomodate 1 soaker in a squatting position. Bathing suit advisable during daylight hours.

No services available on the premises. 2 miles to campground. 14 miles to all other services.

Source maps: Sawtooth National Forest; USGS ·Sydney Butte, Idaho.

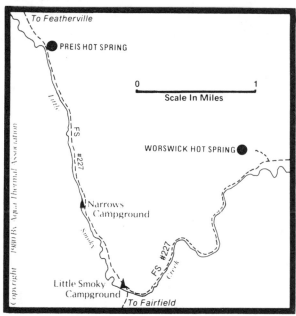

#238   WORSWICK HOT SPRINGS   (see map)
Near the town of Fairfield in Sawtooth National Forest.

Site of historic old resort which has completely deteriorated, returning the hot springs to unimproved status. Elevation 6400 ft. Open all year.

Natural Mineral Water flows out of several springs at temperatures of more than 150 degrees, supplying a series of primitive rock and log pools, in which the water cools to a variety of comfortable temperatures. There is no posted clothing policy, which leaves it up to the mutual consent of those present.

No services on the premises. 2 miles to campground. 14 miles to all other services.

Source maps: Sawtooth National Forest; USGS ·Sydney Butte, Idaho.

▲ *TWIN SPRINGS RESORT: Co-manager Maren demonstrates how to dive into the unique roofless hot pool supplied by a pair of geothermal outflows in the cliffs above the river.*

▶ *This ancient Undershot Pelton wheel, powered by the downhill flow of hot water, still supplies the resort's electricity.*

◀ ▼ *Co-manager Mike adjusts the ordinary lawn sprinkler which sprays the incoming 180 degree water into the air, where it cools to around 100 before the drops hit the surface. Pool temperature is controlled by mixing in hot water as needed.*

#239   TWIN SPRINGS RESORT   (see map)
c/o Atlanta Stage
Boise, ID 83706

Historic old commercial resort and gold mining claim in Boise National Forest. Elevation 3300 ft. Open all year.

Natural Mineral Water flows out of two springs high on the cliffs at a temperature of more than 180 degrees, and is piped to semi-enclosed soaking pool. Hot water is fed to the pool through a fine spray lawn sprinkler, which provides enough cooling effect to maintain the pool temperature between 80 and 100 degrees. The local custom is clothing optional in the pool, and in the river across the road. All buildings are supplied with geothermal heat, and some of the water piped down from the springs turns a Pelton water wheel to generate the electricity used at the resort.

Campground and bar are available at the premises. 45 miles to all other services, including public bus.

Source maps: Boise National Forest; USGS · Twin Springs, Idaho.

#240A   SHEEP CREEK   (see map)
HOT SPRING
On the Boise River in Boise National Forest.

Unimproved hot spring on the south bank of the river. Elevation 3600 ft. Open all year.

Natural Mineral Water flows out of the ground at 120 degrees. Old wooden soaking tub overlooking the river has fallen apart, and may have been replaced by volunteers. Bathing suits advisable.

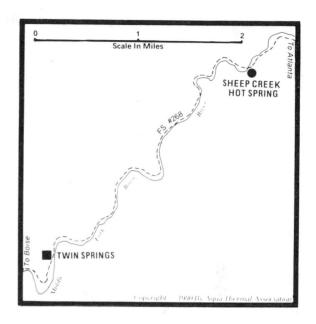

▼ *TWIN SPRING RESORT: Mike and Maren give their dogs some stick-chasing practice in the river after demonstrating the rock-lined primitive hot pools along the bank.*

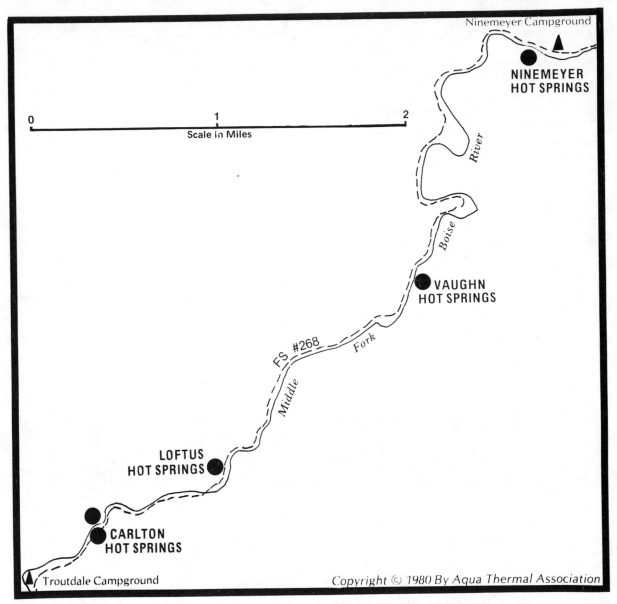

Scale in Miles

Ninemeyer Campground

NINEMEYER
HOT SPRINGS

River

Boise

VAUGHN
HOT SPRINGS

FS #268   Fork

Middle

LOFTUS
HOT SPRINGS

CARLTON
HOT SPRINGS

Troutdale Campground

#240B   CARLTON HOT SPRINGS   *(see map)*
*On the Middle Fork of the Boise River in the Boise
National Forest.*

Two unimproved hot springs, one on each side of the
river. Elevation 3600 ft. Open all year.

Natural Mineral Water flows out of the ground at more
than 120 degrees, into primitive rock pools built by
volunteers at the edge of the river. Temperature controlled by admitting more or less cold river water.

No services on the premises. 48 miles to all services.

Source maps: Boise National Forest; USGS · Sheep
Creek, Idaho.

#240C   LOFTUS HOT SPRING   *(see map)*
On Middle Fork of Boise River in Boise National Forest.

Small unimproved hot spring by the side of the road.
Elevation 3600 ft. Open all year.

Natural Mineral Water flows out of the ground at more
than 120 degrees, into primitive rock pool on hillside
overlooking road and river. Temperature controlled by
diverting hot water flow as desired. Local custom is
clothing optional.

No services available on the premises. 48 miles to all
services.

Source maps: Boise National Forest; USGS Sheep
Creek, Idaho.

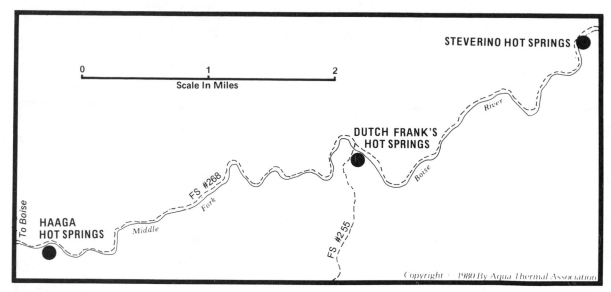

#240D   VAUGHN HOT SPRINGS   (see map)
On the Middle Fork of the Boise River in Boise National Forest.

Unimproved hot spring on south bank of the river. Elevation 3600 ft. Open all year.

Natural Mineral Water flows out of the ground at more than 120 degrees, and plunges over cliff directly into the river. No soaking pools.

No services on the premises. 49 miles to all services.

#241A   NINEMEYER HOT SPRING   (see map)
On the Middle Fork of the Boise River in Boise National Forest.

Several unimproved hot springs on the south bank of the river, across from Ninemeyer Campground. Elevation 3800 ft. Open all year.

Natural Mineral Water flows out of the ground at more than 120 degrees, into primitive rock pools built by volunteers along the edge of the river. It might not be safe to ford river during high water. Springs are directly visible from campground, so bathing suits are advisable during daylight hours.

Campground available on north bank of river. 51 miles to other services.

Source maps: Boise National Forest; USGS - Barber Flat, Idaho.

#241B   HAAGA HOT SPRINGS   (see map)
On the Middle Fork of the Boise River in Boise National Forest.

Several unimproved hot springs on the south bank of the river. Elevation 4000 ft. Open all year.

Natural Mineral Water flows out of several springs at more than 120 degrees, then cascades over a rock ledge directly into the river. No place to build rock soaking pools.

No services on the premises. 51 miles to all services.

Source maps: Boise National Forest; USGS -Grand Mtn. Idaho.

#241C   DUTCH FRANK'S HOT SPRINGS   (see map)
On the Middle Fork of the Boise River in Boise National Forest.

Several unimproved hot springs along a 200 yard stretch of river bank. Elevation 4200 ft. Open all year.

Natural Mineral Water flows out of many openings at more than 120 degrees, supplying primitive rock pools which have been built by volunteers along the edge of the river. All pools are clearly visible from the road, so bathing suits are advisable, at least during daylight hours.

No services available on the premises. 52 miles to all services.

Source maps: Boise National Forest; USGS - Grand Mtn. Idaho.

#241D   STEVERINO HOT SPRINGS   (see map)
On the Middle Fork of the Boise River in Boise National Forest.

Several unimproved hot springs on the north bank of the river. Elevation 4300 ft. Open all year.

Natural Mineral Water flows out of the springs at more than 120 degrees, supplying various primitive rock pools which have been built by volunteers along the edge of the river. All pools are directly visible from the road so bathing suits are advisable, at least during daylight hours.

No services available on the premises. 53 miles to all services.

Source maps: Boise National Forest; USGS - Grand Mtn., Idaho.

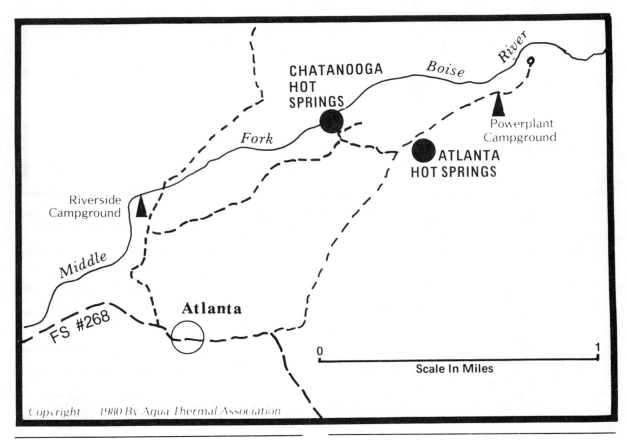

#242A ATLANTA HOT SPRINGS   *(see map)*
Near the historic mining town of Atlanta in Boise National Forest.

Several semi-improved hot springs on a wooded plateau near the Middle Fork of the Boise River. Elevation 5400 ft. Open all year.

Natural Mineral Water flows out of the ground at more than 110 degrees, supplying three natural-bottom soaking pools, small · 107 degrees, medium size · 97 degrees, large · 87 degrees. There is no posted clothing policy, leaving it up to the mutual consent of those present.

No services available on the premises. ½ mile to campground, cabins, restaurant, service station and grocery store. 62 miles to other services.

Source maps: Boise National Forest; USGS · Atlanta East and Atlanta West, Idaho.

#242B CHATANOOGA HOT SPRINGS   *(see map)*
Near the town of Atlanta in Boise National Forest.

Unimproved hot spring on the south bank of the Middle Fork of the Boise River. Elevation 5400 ft. Open all year.

Natural Mineral Water flows out of the ground at more than 120 degrees, and cascades down a cliff into a primitive rock pool built by volunteers. Soaking pool maintains a temperature of approximately 107 degrees, depending on wind and air temperature. There is no posted clothing policy, which leaves it up to the mutual consent of those present.

No services available on the premises. ½ mile to campground, restaurant, cabins, service station and grocery store. 62 miles to other services.

Source maps: Boise National Forest; USGS · Atlanta East and Atlanta West, Idaho.

78

▲ CHATANOOGA HOT SPRINGS: Cascading hot water makes a fine shampoo rinse.

◄ ATLANTA HOT SPRINGS: You can drive within 10 yards of this mystical hot pool.

▲ ROBINSON BAR: *The new creekside sauna building.*

◀ *Hot pool, swim pool and main lodge, with dining patio.*

◀ KEM HOT SPRING: *20 ft. to a level campground.*

◀ SUNBEAM HOT SPRING: *You may fish while soaking.*

#243 **KEM HOT SPRING** *(see map)*
Near the town of Stanley.

Unimproved hot spring on the bank of the Salmon River in the Sawtooth National Recreation Area. Elevation 6100 ft. Open all year.

Natural Mineral Water flows out of the ground at 110 degrees. Volunteers have built several primitive rock pools along the edge of the river. Various temperatures in each pool. Because of visibility from adjoining camping area, bathing suits are advisable, at least in the daytime.

Unofficial camping area immediately adjoining the hot spring. 6 miles to all services. 75 miles to public bus.

Source maps: Sawtooth National Recreation Area.

#244 **SUNBEAM HOT SPRINGS** *(see map)*
Near the town of Stanley.

Numerous flows of very hot water on Forest Service Land flow under the highway (Idaho Route 75) and into the Snake River. Elevation 6000 ft. Open all year.

Natural Mineral Water flows out of the ground at more than 160 degrees. Volunteers have built several primitive rock pools along the edge of the river, where hot and cold mix in a variety of temperatures. As all pools are easily visible from the highway, bathing suits are advisable, at least during daylight hours.

No services available on the premises. 1 mile to all services. 75 miles to public bus.

Source maps: Challis National Forest.

#245 ROBINSON BAR

Clayton, ID 83227

(208) 838-2354
MH

French Restaurant and Inn, located on a mountain ranch, surrounded by Sawtooth National Recreation Area. Elevation 6000 ft. Open June 1 to October 1.

Natural Mineral Water flows out of the ground at 135 degrees. Outdoor swimming pool (no chlorine) · 80 degrees. Outdoor soaking pool (no chlorine) · 107 degrees. Wood fired sauna on bank of cold mountain stream. Clothing optional in pools and sauna areas.

Cabins and haute cuisine restaurant available on the premises. 4 miles to all other services. 80 miles to public bus.

From Idaho Route 75, 2 miles east of Sunbeam, follow signs on gravel road over metal bridge to resort.

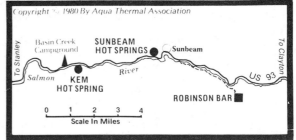

Copyright © 1980 By Aqua Thermal Association

To Stanley — Basin Creek Campground — SUNBEAM HOT SPRINGS — Sunbeam — To Clayton

Salmon — KEM HOT SPRING — River — US 93

ROBINSON BAR

0 1 2 3 4
Scale In Miles

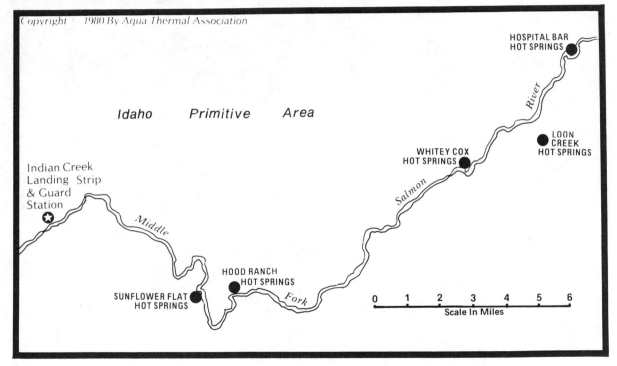

Idaho   Primitive   Area

HOSPITAL BAR
HOT SPRINGS

LOON
CREEK
HOT SPRINGS

WHITEY COX
HOT SPRINGS

Indian Creek
Landing Strip
& Guard
Station

Middle

Salmon   River

HOOD RANCH
HOT SPRINGS

SUNFLOWER FLAT
HOT SPRINGS

Fork

```
0    1    2    3    4    5    6
Scale In Miles
```

#246   CHALLIS HOT SPRINGS

Box 509   (208) 879-4442
Challis, ID 83226   PR + RV

Older resort and community plunge. Elevation 5000 ft. Open all year.

Natural Mineral Water flows out of the ground at 127 degrees. Outdoor pool (no chlorine) · 85 degrees. Indoor pool (no chlorine) · 105 to 110 degrees. Both pools have gravel bottoms. Bathing suits required.

Overnite RV spaces and picnic area available on the premises. No credit cards. 7 miles to all other services, including public bus.

From Challis, go south 3 miles on US 93, then follow signs 4 miles north on paved road to resort.

#247   MIDDLE FORK HOT SPRINGS   (see map)

Located in the Idaho Primitive Area along the Middle Fork of the Salmon River.

Five unimproved hot springs which can be reached only by raft or boat, after being flown in to an upstream raft launching site. Elevation 4000 to 5000 ft. Open during raft season by permit only.

Natural Mineral Water flows out of the ground at various temperatures at Sunflower Camp, Hood Ranch, Whitey Cox, Big Loon and Hospital Bar. The springs take various forms, including a hot waterfall. Each raft trip group determines its own bathing suit policy. The usual custom is clothing optional.

Source maps: Forest Service Map · Middle Fork of the Salmon; Northwest Cartographics · Middle Fork Salmon River.

◀ *CHALLIS HOT SPRINGS: Another would-be diving champ showing off for pictures.*

▼ *PANTHER CREEK HOT SPRINGS: Jump in and die — that water is scalding hot.*

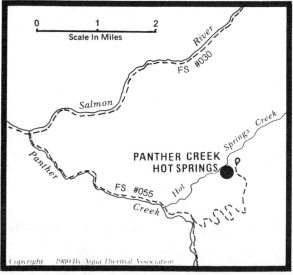

#248 PANTHER CREEK HOT SPRINGS (see map)
Near the town of North Fork.

Dozens of unimproved hot water outflows from the south bank of Warm Springs Creek, in Salmon National Forest. Elevation 4800 ft. Open all year.

Natural Mineral Water flows out of the ground through many openings at more than 170 degrees, toward a series of primitive rock pools which volunteers have built along the bed of Panther Creek. In the winter these pools provide a variety of comfortable temperatures, but in the summer, after the snow has melted, Panther Creek does not carry enough surface water to cool the geothermal water, leaving the pools full of 150 degree water.

No services available on the premises. 33 miles to all services.

Source maps: Salmon National Forest; USGS ·Shoup, Idaho-Montana.

83

HORSE CREEK HOT SPRING: *A rustic roofless bathhouse miles from civilization.*

A cold water dip is just 50 ft. away.

The pool is a cozy size for four people.

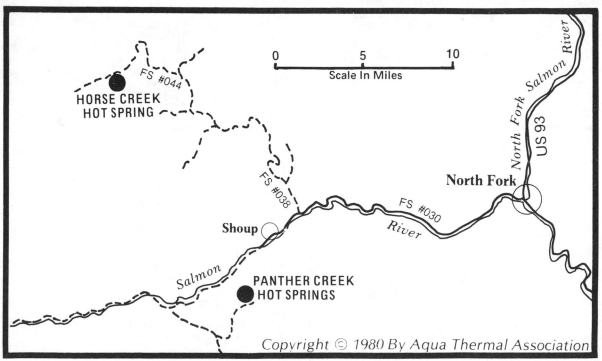

HORSE CREEK HOT SPRING

FS #044

FS #038

FS #030

Shoup

North Fork

North Fork Salmon River

US 93

Salmon River

PANTHER CREEK HOT SPRINGS

0   5   10
Scale In Miles

> ◀ *RUSSIAN JOHN HOT SPRING: Idyllic and easily accessible. Too bad the water isn't at least 10 degrees warmer.*

#249 HORSE CREEK HOT SPRING   *(see map)*
Near the town of North Fork.

Small bathhouse built over primitive hot spring in Salmon National Forest, adjoining picnic grounds, and mountain stream. Elevation 6200 ft. Open all year.

Natural Mineral Water flows out of the ground at 97 degrees, directly into primitive rock pool surrounded by roofless bathhouse. There is no posted clothing policy, leaving it up to the mutual consent of those present.

Picnic area, with tables and rest rooms, available at the spring. Campground 1 mile. 35 miles to all services.

Source maps: Salmon National Forest.

#250 RUSSIAN JOHN HOT SPRING   *(see map)*
Near the town of Ketchum.

Remains of old sheepherder pool on National Forest Land, 100 yards from Idaho Route 75. Elevation 6900 ft. Open all year.

Natural Mineral Water flows out of the ground at 89 degrees, into small clay bottom pool, which maintains a temperature of no more than 86 degrees. Local custom is clothing optional in the pool.

No services available on the premises. 16 miles to all services.

Source maps: USGS · Easley Hot Springs, Idaho.

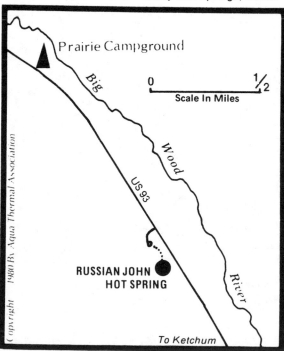

#251   WARFIELD HOT SPRING   (see map)
Near the town of Ketchum.

Non-commercial old bathhouse on Forest Service land in Warm Springs Canyon. Elevation 6400 ft. Open all year.

Natural Mineral Water flows out of the ground from two springs at 97 and 102 degrees, supplying two individual tubs in bathhouse. Bathing suits not required in bathhouse rooms.

No services available on the premises. 11 miles to all services.

Source maps: USGS - Griffin Butte, Idaho.

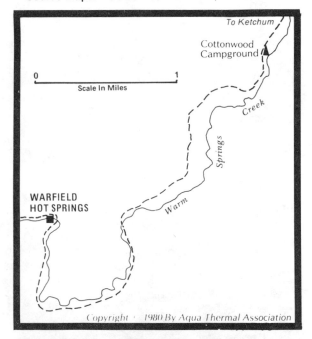

▲ THE HOT SPOT: The first rent-a-tub establishment in Idaho, but not the last.

◄ WARFIELD HOT SPRING: Neglected but not vandalized. Funky — and it's free.

#252 THE HOT SPOT
312 East Ave. North   *(208) 726-3444*
Ketchum, ID 83340   *PR*

Rent-a-tub establishment in Ketchum business district. Elevation 6000 ft. Open all year.

Gas-heated city water. Six enclosed (no roof) wooden hot tubs with hydrojets - 102 degrees. Bathing suits not required in pool enclosures.

3 blocks to motel, restaurant, grocery store and service station. 1 mile to full hook-up RV spaces, picnic area and public bus.

#253 BALD MOUNTAIN HOT SPRINGS
Box 426 (South Main Street)   *(208) 726-9963*
Ketchum, ID 83340   *PR + MH*

Older motel with Olympic size pool in Ketchum business district. Elevation 6000 ft. Open all year, except pool open only from Memorial Day to Labor Day.

Natural Mineral Water piped in from Guyer Hot Spring, 3 miles up Hot Springs Canyon. Outdoor swimming pool - 88 to 92 degrees. Outdoor soaking pool - controllable temperature. Bathing suits required.

Rooms available on the premises. VISA and Mastercharge accepted. 2 blocks to restaurant, grocery store and service station. 1 mile to full hook-up RV spaces and public bus.

#254 ELKHORN AT SUN VALLEY
Box 1067   *(208) 622-4511*
Sun Valley, ID 83353   *Hydrotherapy Pool   MH*

THE HOT SPOT: Each group renting a private patio has the freedom to set its own rules on clothing, champagne, or games.

BALD MOUNTAIN HOT SPRINGS: A warm water swim pool with a view of ski slopes.

Showing original bath house over hot springs and hot pool bathing, lodge. About 1910

▲ HEISE HOT SPRINGS: An historic photo of how the place looked 70 years ago.

◄ The big swim pool, bath house and sun deck.

▼ The soaking pool and adjoining all-year swim pool, in a nearby part of the grounds.

▼ The sign of a continuously growing resort.

#255   HEISE HOT SPRINGS
Box 417   (208) 538-7312
Ririe, ID 83443   PR + RV

   Modernized family-oriented resort with spacious tree-shaded picnic and RV grounds. Elevation 5000 ft. Open all year.
   Natural Mineral Water flows out of the ground at 120 degrees. Outdoor soaking pool (no chlorine) · 106 degrees. Two outdoor swimming pools use municipal water, geothermally heated. Large pool (open May 14 to September 15) · 85 degrees. Smaller pool (open all year) ·95 degrees. Bathing suits required.
   Restaurant, picnic area, golf course and full hook-up RV spaces available on the premises. No credit cards. 5 miles to grocery store and service station. 18 miles to motel and public bus.
   From the town of Idaho Falls, go east 15 miles on US 26. Follow signs north across river to resort.

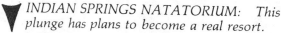

GREEN CANYON HOT SPRINGS: The big indoor pool is flanked by game machines.

INDIAN SPRINGS NATATORIUM: This plunge has plans to become a real resort.

#256 GREEN CANYON HOT SPRINGS
Box 96   (208) 458-4454
Newdale, ID 83436   PR + RV

Rural indoor plunge and picnic grounds. Elevation 6000 ft. Open Easter to week after Labor Day.

Natural Mineral Water flows out of the ground at 118 degrees. Indoor swimming pool · 80 to 90 degrees. Bathing suits required. Geothermal greenhouse produces hydroponic tomatoes and cucumbers.

Picnic area and full hook-up RV spaces available on the premises. 21 miles to all other services, including public bus.

From the town of Driggs, go west 17 miles on Idaho Route 33. At Canyon Creek Bridge, turn south and follow signs 4 miles to resort.

#257A OXBOW MOTOR INN
4333 Yellowstone Ave.
Pocatello, ID 83201   (208) 237-3100
                                   Hydrojet Pool   MH

#257B BEST WESTERN COTTONTREE INN
1415 Pocatello Bench Rd.
Pocatello, ID 83201   (208) 237-7650
                                   Hydrojet Pool   MH

#258 INDIAN SPRINGS NATATORIUM
Box 366   (208) 226-2174
American Falls, ID 83211   PR + RV

Older rural picnic ground and plunge. Elevation 5200 ft. Open April 1 to Labor Day.

Natural Mineral Water flows out of the ground at 90 degrees. Outdoor swimming pool · 90 degrees. No chlorine. Bathing suits required.

Picnic area and full hook-up RV spaces available on the premise. No credit cards. 3 miles to all other services, including public bus.

Located on Idaho Route 37, 3 miles south of the town of American Falls.

LAVA HOT SPRINGS RESORT: These modern structures, used by the elderly, replaced the old wooden bathhouses.

Young people prefer these city-water pools built on the other edge of the town.

▲ *LAVA HOT SPRINGS RESORT: The first bathhouse, erected sometime before 1900.*

▶ *SODA SPRINGS: One of several mineral water outflows well known to travelers on the Oregon Trail. The output from Beer Springs was reputed to have the flavor of a lager beer, but unfortunately it was flat.*

#259A LAVA HOT SPRINGS RESORT
Box 387   (208) 776-5254
Lava Hot Springs, ID 83246   PR

Modern health center operated by the Lava Hot Springs Foundation, a self-supporting state agency, on the main street in town. Elevation 5500 ft. Hot pools open all year. Swimming pool open May 1 through Labor Day.

Natural Mineral Water flows out of the ground at 110 degrees. Two outdoor soaking pools · 104 to 110 degrees. Two outdoor jet pools · 104 degrees. Eight private rooms with individual tubs and steam baths. Bathing suits required except in private rooms.

Picnic area and massage available on the premises. No credit cards. 3 blocks to all other services, including public bus.

From Interstate 15, go 11 miles east on US 30 to the town of Lava Hot Springs.

#259B HOME HOTEL AND MOTEL
317 E. Main St.   (208) 776-5507
Lava Hot Springs, ID 83246   MH

Older hotel with motel wing on the main street of town. Elevation 5400 ft. Open all year.

Natural Mineral Water flows out of the ground at 126 degrees, and is piped to bathrooms of hotel and motel units, some with oversize tubs.

Rooms available on the premises. VISA and Mastercharge accepted. 2 blocks to all other services, including public bus.

From Interstate 15, go 11 miles east on US 30 to the town of Lava Hot Springs.

#260 SODA (HOOPER) SPRINGS
Near the town of Soda Springs

Naturally carbonated cold water spring surrounded by tree-shaded picnic area. Elevation 5200 ft. Open all year.

Natural Mineral Water flows out of the ground at 54 degrees into open pool where many people fill their jugs with supplies of "soda water". The original source of local hot mineral water, "Steamboat Spring", was drowned under a nearby reservoir when it was built.

From US 30, in the center of the town of Soda Springs, follow signs north to public park with soda spring.

#261 DOWNATTA HOT SPRINGS
Route 1   *(208) 897-5736*
Downey, ID 83234   *PR + RV*

Older rural plunge and picnic grounds being remodeled and expanded. Elevation 4000 ft. Open all year.

Natural Mineral Water flows out of the ground at 112 degrees. Outdoor swimming pool · 80 to 90 degrees. Six outdoor wooden hot tubs · 106 degrees. No chlorine in pool or tubs. Bathing suits required.

Picnic area and full hook-up RV spaces available on the premises. No credit cards. 3 miles to grocery store and service station. 12 miles to restaurant, motel and public bus.

Located on US 91, 3 miles south of the town of Downey.

#262 DEL RIO HOT SPRINGS
near the town of Preston.

Abandoned artesian well and buildings which have been a resort, a poultry hatchery, a greenhouse and a slaughterhouse.

Natural Mineral Water flows out of the well at over 200 degrees, with a concentrated mineral content that builds up rapidly as the water cools. There are no pools suitable for personal soaking.

No services are available on the premises.

From the center of Preston, take Dayton Road across river to Hot Spring Road, the first road on the right, then turn north. Buildings and mineral deposits are visible on both sides of the road.

#263 BEAR LAKE HOT SPRINGS
Box 75   *(208) 945-2494*
St. Charles, ID 83272   *PR + RV*

Large pool building and campground on remote section of lakeshore. Elevation 6000 ft. Open April to October.

Natural Mineral Water flows out of the ground at 115 degrees. Indoor swimming pool · 75 to 80 degrees. Indoor soaking pool · 110 degrees. Bathing suits required.

Lake beachfront, picnic area, cafe, and overnite RV spaces available on the premises. No credit cards. 6 miles to service station. 17 miles to all other services, including public bus.

From US 89, on north side of St. Charles, follow signs east across north end of lake to resort.

▲ *DOWNATTA HOT SPRINGS: Official signs with heavy messages are delivered with a light touch and a sense of humor.*

▶ *BEAR LAKE HOT SPRINGS: This resort has a short season even with an indoor pool.*

★DOWNATTA HOT SPRINGS: *Slides, floats and rings make this an active swimming pool.*

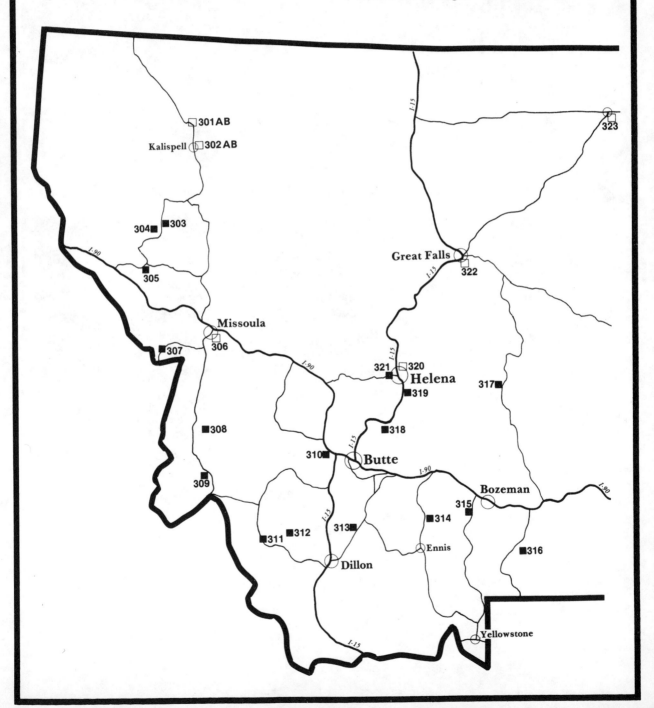

● Unimproved Mineral Water Locations
■ Improved Mineral Water Locations
□ City Water Establishments

REGIONAL KEY MAP

Each location has been assigned a location number, and Directory listings have been arranged numerically.

301 AB

Kalispell 302 AB

304■ 303

305

Missoula
306

307

Great Falls
322

308

321■ 320
Helena
319

317■

318

310■ Butte

309

Bozeman
315

314

311 312

313

316

Ennis

Dillon

Yellowstone

323

I-15

I-90

I-15

I-15

I-90

I-90

I-15

I-90

I-15

MONTANA:

Big Business Under the Big Sky

The rolling hills and plains of eastern Montana have no hot springs at all. All of Montana's geothermal action is concentrated in the mountainous western portion, but you won't find any publicly-owned, poetic, hot mineral pools to loll in. Instead, you will find a wide variety of hot spring business establishments, some with asking prices in the millions.

Fairmont Hot Springs Resort, west of Anaconda, typifies maximum development, with large outdoor and indoor pools, resort rooms, convention rooms, restaurant, cocktail bar with dancing, tennis courts, golf course, riding stables, fishing, skiing and snowmobiling in season, and condominiums for sale.

Chico Hot Springs, 30 miles north of Yellowstone, is older, small and more rustic, without condominiums, yet still big enough to handle conventions of 300. Lolo Hot Springs, near the Idaho border, has the basic pools, motel, bar, restaurant, RV park and saddle horses, plus a big new rodeo grounds. Broadwater Athletic Club and Hot Spring, on the west edge of Helena, consists of a new brick building large enough to hold an indoor running track in addition to all kinds of fitness equipment rooms, saunas, steam rooms and mineral water pools.

Not all the Montana hot springs have made it to the big time — at least not yet — but

SLEEPING CHILD HOT SPRINGS . . . . . page 101

95

every one has its plans, or at least dreams, for expansion. In some cases, nothing less than a new owner with the courage to tear out the old buildings and pools and start over, will enable a tired and tattered relic from the past to be born anew. At the same time, there is little likelihood that any of the geothermal outflows will be abandoned and return to their natural state, available without charge to anyone. Even hot springs far from population centers are perceived to have big economic potentials, as soon as they can be exploited.

Camp Aqua, Montana's northernmost natural mineral water resort, deserves special mention. The unpretentious grounds contain only a few cabins, a full hook-up RV section and a simple one-story bathhouse, with no swimming pools or condominiums. However, the owner departed from traditional hot spring architecture by not building separate men's and women's sections in the bathhouse. Instead, he anticipated the popularity of urban rent-a-tub establishments by providing individual private rooms large enough for 8 people. Each room contains a toilet, a sauna, and a steam room in addition to a large flow-through soaking pool. Although not fancy, this is about the only chance you will have to go skinny-dipping as a couple or family in natural, unchlorinated mineral water in the state of Montana.

FAIRMONT HOT SPRINGS . . . . page 102

Geothermal Energy

Until the 1960s it was more efficient to install a propane tank, or connect to a natural gas line, than to fight the corrosion problems of installing geothermal space heating, even on the grounds of a hot spring resort. In recent years the development of impervious plastic pipe, and skyrocketing petroleum prices, have combined to stimulate the use of geothermal heat in new construction. Fairmont, Broadwater, Camp Aqua and Jackson Hot Springs are examples of this new appreciation.

At Warm Springs State Hospital a DOE-funded demonstration project is under way, designed to provide geothermal heat to the hospital buildings. A new well will be drilled near the historic old spring, which has been kept tightly covered for many years to prevent patients from accidentally drowning themselves.

Preliminary studies have begun for expanding the small private geothermal system that serves two buildings in White Sulphur Springs; for constructing greenhouses and fish tanks at Chico Hot Springs; and for the construction of a demonstration methanol plant near Silverstar.

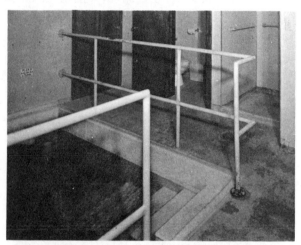

The following codes were used in the preparation of listings and maps on the following pages.

NATURAL MINERAL WATER LOCATIONS ARE SET IN BOLD TYPE — like this
GAS HEATED CITY WATER LOCATIONS ARE SET IN REGULAR TYPE — like this

PR = Tubs or pools for rent, by hour, day or treatment.
MH = Rooms or cabins for rent by day, week or month.
RV = Vehicle spaces for rent by day, week, month, or year.

Open all year means that there are no doors or gates closed during a part of the year. However, snow or high water may temporarily make the location inaccessible.

————— Paved highway
— — — — Gravel or dirt road
·····⋅·····⋅ Hiking trail
▲ Campground

#301A PTARMIGAN VILLAGE
Box 4444
Whitefish, MT 59937

(406) 862-3594
Hydrojet Pool MH

#301B VIKING LODGE
Box 298
Whitefish, MT 59937

(406) 862-3547
Whirlpool MH

#302A BEST WESTERN OUTLAW INN
1701 Hwy 93 South
Kalispell, MT 59901

(406) 755-6100
Whirlpool MH

#302B FOUR SEASONS MOTOR INN
350 N. Main St.
Kalispell, MT 59901

(406) 755-6123
Whirlpool MH

#303 CAMP AQUA
Box 592
Hot Springs, MT 59845

(406) 741-3480
PR + RV + MH

Well-maintained family rent-a-tub establishment, with overnight facilities, surrounded by rolling foothills. Elevation 4000 ft. Open all year.

Natural Mineral Water flows out of artesian well at 124 degrees. Six individual indoor soaking pools in private rooms, each with steam bath, sauna and toilet. Temperature controllable to 110 degrees. Bathing suits not required in private rooms. Geothermal heat used in all buildings.

Cabins, full hook-up RV spaces and picnic area available on the premises. 6 miles to all other services, including public bus.

From Montana Route 28, 2½ miles north of Hot Springs Junction, follow signs east two miles on gravel road to resort.

▲ CAMP AQUA: *Water flow and temperature is controllable within each private room.*

#304 CAMAS HOT SPRINGS
(406)   741-2473
Hot Springs, MT 59845   PR + RV

Large health center owned and operated by the Flathead Indian Tribes, in rolling foothills near the Bitterroot River. Elevation 4000 ft. Open all year, except outdoor pool open from Memorial Day to Labor Day.

Natural Mineral Water flows out of the ground at 104 degrees. Outdoor swimming pool · 83 degrees. Indoor mens and womens bathhouses, each with 6 individual tubs, mud bath, steam bath and sweat room. Bathing suits required except in bathhouses.

Chiropractor, massage and overnight RV spaces available on the premises. VISA and Mastercharge accepted. 3 miles to all other services, including public bus.

Four miles north of junction of Montana Route 28 and Route 382, follow signs two miles west to resort.

#305 QUINN'S HOT SPRINGS
Box 187   (406) 826-3432
Paradise, MT 59856

RV campground and resort in a tree-lined canyon along the Clark Fork River. Elevation 2700 ft. Open all year except pools open during summer only.

Natural Mineral Water flows out of the ground at 107 degrees. Outdoor jet pool · 105 degrees. Gas-heated city water in the swimming pool · 80 degrees. Bathing suits required.

Restaurant, bar, picnic area and full hook-up RV spaces available on the premises. No credit cards. 100 yards to fishing stream. 4 miles to grocery store and service station. 10 miles to motel. 20 miles to public bus.

Located on Montana Route 135, 3 miles south of the junction with Montana Route 200.

#306 VILLAGE RED LION MOTOR INN
100 Madison St.   (406) 728-3100
Missoula, MT 59801   Hydrojet Pool   MH

▲ *CAMAS HOT SPRINGS: Men are assigned to one floor, women monopolize the other.*

▼ *QUINN'S HOT SPRINGS: One of the few resorts with hydrojets in an outdoor pool.*

#307   LOLO HOT SPRINGS   (406) Missoula Operator
RESORT   for Lolo Hot Springs Line 1
Lolo, MT 59847   PR + RV + MH

Expanding resort surrounded by Lolo National Forest. Elevation 4200 ft. Open all year.

Natural Mineral Water flows out of the ground at 140 degrees. Outdoor swimming pool - 75 to 82 degrees. Indoor soaking pool - 104 degrees. Bathing suits required.

Rooms, restaurant, grocery store, service station, picnic ground, full hook-up RV spaces, and fishing available on the premises. VISA and Mastercharge accepted. 35 miles to public bus.

Located on US 12, 25 miles west of junction with US 93.

◄ *LOLO HOT SPRINGS: Poolside boulders set off the mountain valley location of this rapidly expanding commercial resort.*

▼ *During the summer months the indoor hot pool is not as busy as during the winter.*

▲ *SLEEPING CHILD SPRINGS:*
Refreshments at poolside.

▶ *Rustic buildings fit the scenery.*

▼ *MEDICINE HOT SPRING:*
Mountain-style summer resort.

#308   SLEEPING CHILD HOT SPRINGS
Box 768   (406) 363-9910
Hamilton, MT 59840   PR + RV + MH

A small resort designed to provide "rustic elegance", surrounded by Lolo National Forest.

Natural Mineral Water flows out of the ground at 125 degrees. Outdoor swimming pool · 99 degrees. Outdoor soaking pool · 110 degrees. Outdoor jet pool · 115 degrees. One indoor sauna. Bathing suits required.

Rooms, restaurant, bar and overnite RV spaces available on the premises. VISA and Mastercharge accepted. 13 miles to all other services, including public bus.

From the town of Hamilton, take US 93 south to Montana Route 38, then east to Montana Route 501. Follow signs south to resort.

#309   MEDICINE HOT SPRINGS RESORT
                                            (406) 821-3558
Conner, MT 59827   PR + RV + MH

Older resort surrounded by Bitterroot National Forest. Elevation 4500 ft. Open April through October.

Natural Mineral Water flows out of the ground at 129 degrees. Outdoor swimming pool · 100 degrees or more. Three individual tubs in private rooms · controllable to 110 degrees. Bathing suits required except in private rooms.

Cabins, overnite RV spaces and picnic area available on the premises. No credit cards. Two miles to all other services. 60 miles to public bus.

#310 FAIRMONT HOT SPRINGS RESORT

(406) 797-3241

Anaconda, MT 59711

Major new all-year resort and real estate develop-ment. Elevation 5300 ft. Open all year.

Natural Mineral Water flows out of the ground at 160 + degrees. Outdoor swimming pool - 80 to 85 degrees. Outdoor soaking pool - 108 to 110 degrees. Indoor swimming pool - 80 to 85 degrees. Indoor soaking pool - 108 to 110 degrees. Men's and women's locker rooms each contain a sauna. Bathing suits required except in saunas. Geothermal heat in all buildings.

Rooms, restaurant, golf, tennis, game room, and mini zoo on the premises. VISA, Mastercharge and American Express accepted. 1 block to full hook-up RV spaces. 5 miles to grocery store and service station. 15 miles to public bus.

From Interstate 90, 12 miles west of Butte, take Fairmont Hot Springs exit and follow signs to resort.

#311 JACKSON HOT SPRINGS LODGE

Box 808   (406) 834-2141

Jackson, MT 59736   PR + RV + MH

Historic resort being restored to full operation. Elevation 5200 ft. Open all year.

Natural Mineral Water flows out of the ground at 137 degrees. Indoor swimming pool - 98 to 100 degrees. 5 rooms in lodge with hot mineral water piped to bathtubs. No chlorine in any of the mineral water, which is also used to heat the building. Bathing suits required.

Rooms, restaurant, and full hook-up RV spaces available on the premises. No credit cards. 1 block to grocery store and service station. 48 miles to public bus.

Located on Montana Route 278 in the town of Jackson.

#312 ELKHORN HOT SPRINGS

(406) 834-2416

Polaris, MT 59746   PR + RV + MH

All year commercial resort surrounded by Beaverhead National Forest. Elevation 7400 ft. Open all year.

Natural Mineral Water flows out of the ground from two springs at 107 and 160 degrees. Outdoor swimming pool - 88 degrees. Outdoor soaking pool - 98 degrees. Separate men's and women's bathhouses with roman bath and sauna in each. Bathing suits required except in bathhouses.

Rooms, restaurant, grocery store, service station, full hook-up RV spaces, tent spaces and picnic area available on the premises. Hunting, fishing, back packing, skiing, etc. available nearby. Pick-up service provided from Butte. 43 miles to public bus.

From the town of Jackson on Montana Route 278 go east 17 miles, then follow signs 13 miles north to resort.

#313 NEW BILTMORE HOT SPRING

Drawer P   (406) 684-5429

Twin Bridges, MT 59754   PR + RV

Older rural resort with large riverside tree-shaded campground. Elevation 5000 ft. Open all year.

Natural Mineral Water flows out of the ground at 131 degrees. Indoor swimming pool - 80 degrees in summer, 100 degrees in winter. Two individual indoor tubs, con-trollable up to 110 degrees. Bathing suits required except in individual tubs.

Overnite RV spaces, picnic area and fishing available on the premises. No credit cards. 8 miles to all other services. 20 miles to public bus.

From the town of Twin Bridges, go 7 1/2 miles south on Montana Route 41, then follow signs 4 1/2 miles west on gravel road to resort.

◄ **FAIRMONT HOT SPRINGS RESORT:**
The outdoor pools are surrounded
by large and luxurious buildings.

▲ The indoor pool will hold hundreds.

▼ A billiard room commands a view
of the indoor hot and cool pools.

► **JACKSON HOT
SPRINGS LODGE:**
Conventional size
indoor swim pool in
one wing of lodge.

**NEW BILTMORE
HOT SPRING:**
Older and smaller
rural indoor pool. ▼

#314 BEAR TRAP HOT SPRINGS
Box 24   (406) 685-3303
Norris, MT 59745   PR + RV

RV park in rolling country below the Tobacco Root Mountains. Elevation 5000 ft. Open all year.

Natural Mineral Water flows out of the ground at 128 degrees. Outdoor soaking pool · 101 degrees in summer, 106 degrees in winter. Flow-through mineral water · no chlorine. Bathing suits required. Skinny dipping club is active during winter and evenings.

Grocery store, picnic area and full hook-up RV spaces available on the premises. No credit cards. ¼ mile to service station. 10 miles to motel. 17 miles to restaurant. 32 miles to public bus.

From US 287 in the town of Norris, go ¼ mile east on Montana Route 84.

#315 BOZEMAN HOT SPRINGS
Rte. 4, Box 142 Lower Rainbow Road   (406) 587-3030
Bozeman, MT 59715   PR + RV

KOA campground with mineral water pools. Elevation 4500 ft. Open all year. Pools closed from sundown Friday to sundown Saturday.

Natural Mineral Water flows out of the ground at 141 degrees. Indoor swimming pool · 90 degrees. Indoor soaking pools · 112, 110, and 105 degrees. Indoor cold pool · 60 degrees. Bathing suits required.

Grocery store, full hook-up RV spaces, picnic area, and tent trailer rentals available on the premises. No credit cards. ½ mile to restaurant and service station. 8 miles to motel and public bus.

Located on US 191, 8 miles southwest of the town of Bozeman.

#316 CHICO HOT SPRINGS LODGE   (406) 333-4411
Pray, MT 59065   PR + RV + MH

Large older resort surrounded by Gallatin National Forest. Elevation 5000 ft. Open all year.

Natural Mineral Water flows out of the ground at 110 degrees. Outdoor swimming pool · 90 degrees. Outdoor soaking pool · 108 degrees. Flow-through mineral water in both pools · no chlorine. Bathing suits required.

Rooms, restaurant, bar, full hook-up RV spaces, tent spaces, picnic grounds, private trout lake, and saddle horses available on the premises. Visa and Master Charge accepted. 4 miles to grocery store and service station. 26 miles to public bus.

From US 89 take Montana Route 362 for 3 miles. Follow signs to resort.

► CHICO HOT SPRINGS: *Open air swim pool and roofed-over hot pool are a compromise with the weather at this mile-high resort.*

◄ BEAR TRAP HOT SPRINGS: *This rural pool has air-cooled flow-through hot water.*

#317   SPA MOTEL & RESTAURANT   (406) 547-3366
Box 370
White Sulphur Springs, MT 59645   PR + MH

Remodeled older resort at the foot of the Castle Mountains. Elevation 5060 ft. Open all year.

Natural Mineral Water flows out of the ground at 135 degrees. Outdoor swimming pool - 94 degrees in summer, 105 degrees in winter. Indoor soaking pool - 106 to 108 degrees. Flow-through mineral water in both pools -no chlorine. Bathing suits required.

Rooms, restaurant and picnic area available on the premises. Visa and Mastercharge accepted. 1 mile to all other services. 120 miles to public bus.

Located on US 89 at the west end of White Sulphur Springs.

#318   BOULDER HOT SPRINGS   (406) 225-9996
(406) 225-4272
Boulder, MT 59632   PR + RV + MH

Historic older resort being remodeled. Elevation 5000 ft., overlooking the Elkhorn Mountain Range. Open all year.

Natural Mineral Water flows out of the ground at 175 degrees. Outdoor swimming pool - 80 to 100 degrees. Two indoor soaking pools - 110 degrees. One indooor cold plunge - 65 to 70 degrees. One steam bath. Bathing suits required except in private rooms.

Rooms and full hook-up RV spaces available on the premises. No credit cards. 3 miles to all other services, including public bus.

From Interstate 15, take Boulder exit, then south on Montana Route 69 for three miles from the town of Boulder. Turn right on short gravel road to resort.

#319   HILLBROOK NURSING HOME
Clancy, MT 59634
(406) 933-8311

Skilled intermediate nursing facility qualified for Medicaid and Medicare. Elevation 5000 ft. Open all year.

Natural Mineral Water flows out of the ground at 147 degrees. One indoor tub with air jets for treatment. All buildings supplied with geothermal heat.

Admission on doctor's orders only. Information brochure available on request. No credit cards.

From Interstate 15, take Clancy exit, then south 1 mile on frontage road.

#320   SHILO INN
2020 Prospect Ave.   (406) 442-0320
Helene, MT 59601   Hydrojet Pool   MH

#321   BROADWATER ATHLETIC CLUB & HOT SPRING
Box 884   (406) 443-5777
Helena, MT 59601

Newly constructed health center near Helena. Elevation 5000 ft. Open all year.

Natural Mineral Water flows out of the ground at 153 degrees. Outdoor soaking pool - 105 degrees. Indoor swimming pool - 85 degrees. Men's and women's bathhouses, each containing a steam bath, sauna and jet pool - 108 degrees. Bathing suits required in pools; not in bathhouses. Public admitted to swimming pool; other facilities for club members only.

Racquetball and indoor running track on the premises. 2 miles to all other services, including public bus.

Located on US 12, two miles west of the city of Helena.

#322   SHERATON INN
400 10th Ave. S.   (406) 727-7200
Great Falls, MT 59405   Hydrojet Pool   MH

#323   KOA OF HAVRE
(406) 265-5012
Havre, MT 59501   Therapy Pool   RV

▲ BROADWATER ATHLETIC CLUB: The new building is still under construction.

◀ HILLBROOK NURSING HOME: One of the few medical facilities located at a hot spring.

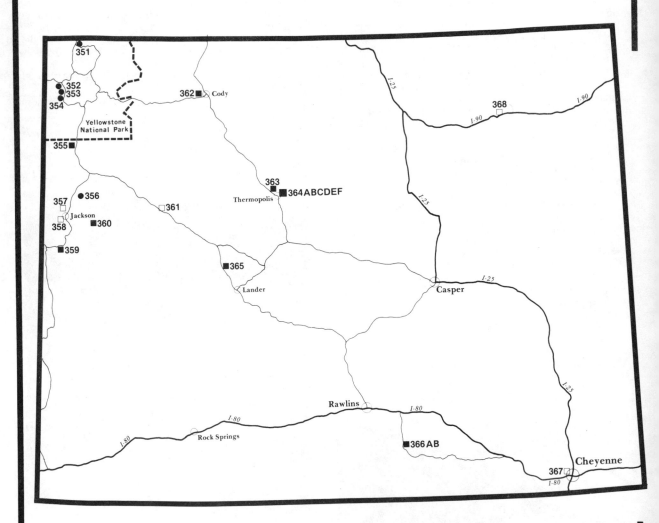

REGIONAL KEY MAP

● Unimproved Mineral Water Locations
■ Improved Mineral Water Locations
□ City Water Establishments

351
352
353
354

362 ■ Cody

368 □

I-25
I-90
I-90

Yellowstone
National Park

355 ■

363
364 ABCDEF
Thermopolis

I-25

357 □
● 356

361 □

Jackson

358 □
■ 360

I-25

359 ■

■ 365

Lander
Casper

I-25

Rawlins
I-80

I-80
I-80

Rock Springs
■ 366 AB

I-25

367 □ Cheyenne

I-80

Each location has been assigned a location number,
and Directory listings have been arranged numerically.

WYOMING:

The Use and Misuse of "Holy" Water

In Wyoming the hot mineral water situation is, to say the least, bizarre. Consider these three situations:

1. In the town of Midwest, in Natrona County, private interests have drilled deep wells into sedimentary rock, bringing up 15,000 gallons per minute of 200 degree water, which is then used for enhanced oil recovery. As of 1979 this one enterprise represented 90% of all of the commercial geothermal activity in the entire Western United States, excluding California.

2. The town of Thermopolis has grown up around the one square mile Thermopolis State Park, where a natural hot spring delivers millions of gallons of 135 degree water each day. The State Park has several hotels, multi-pool public plunges, a hospital, a rehabilitation center and a home for older citizens of Wyoming. Hot water from the main spring is piped to all of these buildings for use in pools and therapy tubs, but geothermal space heating is not used in any of them, nor is any water piped into the adjoining town of Thermopolis. Until recently, the State of Wyoming has refused permission for the town to utilize this hot water supply.

3. In Yellowstone National Park, owned and operated by the Interior Department of the Federal Government, millions of gallons of steaming hot thermal water gush from the ground every day in several different geyser

BOILING RIVER . . . . page 110

MIDWAY BASIN BRIDGE . . . . page 112 ▼ STAR PLUNGE . . . . page 116

basins, and then flow across the ground to disappear into nearby cold water streams. At the same time, thousands of gallons of oil are burned each day to heat space and reservoir water in the many hotels, restaurants, commercial enterprises, administration buildings, school buildings and residences of National Park employees. By the end of 1979 not only was there zero use of geothermal heat in any of these buildings, but no one had even considered the possibility. In fact, the very idea of anyone making such a study was officially dismissed as being *unthinkable*.

What ironies! Private enterprise drills deep for geothermal water where none is visible on the surface, and then uses that water to help produce more oil, while state and federal officials procrastinate about making any constructive use of their free flowing "holy" water, meanwhile burning thousands of gallons of oil.

There is one small consolation at Thermopolis State Park. There, visitors are at least permitted to do more than just gaze at the colorful pools and algae formations deposited over the years by the hot mineral water. The State of Wyoming provides a free bathhouse with both indoor and outdoor soaking pools. Also, as mentioned above, hot mineral water is piped to the nearby commercial plunges and hotel pools, serving hundreds of families every day.

On the other hand, in Yellowstone National Park, officials have made it illegal for anyone to bathe in any kind of thermal water before that water joins with a surface stream. Then, if more than a dozen people do try to bathe at such a place in a stream, the officials arbitrarily declare it closed on the grounds that "the visual impact of those bathers is offensive to some of the non-bathing tourists." Furthermore, absolutely no thought or effort is being given toward channeling any portion of all that geothermal run-off into pools where visitors could soak their weary muscles. As a result, those visitors now have no choice but to return to the four thousand hotel rooms in Yellowstone Park hotels, and soak in a bathtub of reservoir water heated by an oil-burning boiler. Any suggestion that a study be made toward assisting visitors to bathe in the naturally heated thermal water is officially dismissed as being *unthinkable*.

Fortunately, not all Wyoming's geothermal resources are controlled by the same bureaucratic blind men. In Saratoga, the historic old Hobo Spring has been channelled into a well-maintained 107 degree soaking pool, available to all without charge; a charge is made for the use of an adjoining full size municipal swimming pool. At Granite Hot Spring, in a National Forest Canyon south of Jackson, a small charge is made for the use of a large hillside soaking pool maintained at 100 degrees in the summer and 110 degrees in the winter. At Fort Washakie, two Indian tribes have cooperated to build a large plunge and bathhouse which is free to tribe members, and available to non-Indians for a fee.

Geothermal Energy

None of the commercial hot spring establishments in Wyoming make use of geothermal energy for space heating or other commercial applications. However, DOE-funded exploratory drilling has begun near Cody, and studies have started on the use of geothermal heating in the town of Thermopolis, using hot mineral water from the adjoining State Park.

None of the federal or state study programs include Yellowstone National Park. The people at Yellowstone not only refuse to think about utilizing the vast amounts of energy going to waste in that Park, they apparently don't want anyone else to do any thinking about it either.

The following codes were used in the preparation of listings and maps on the following pages.

NATURAL MINERAL WATER LOCATIONS ARE SET IN BOLD TYPE — like this
GAS HEATED CITY WATER LOCATIONS ARE SET IN REGULAR TYPE — like this

PR = *Tubs or pools for rent, by hour, day or treatment.*
MH = *Rooms or cabins for rent by day, week or month.*
RV = *Vehicle spaces for rent by day, week, month, or year.*

Open all year means that there are no doors or gates closed during a part of the year. However, snow or high water may temporarily make the location inaccessible.

————— Paved highway
— — — — Gravel or dirt road
·············· Hiking trail
▲ Campground

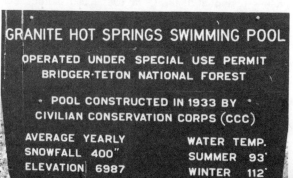

GRANITE HOT SPRINGS SWIMMING POOL
OPERATED UNDER SPECIAL USE PERMIT
BRIDGER-TETON NATIONAL FOREST

POOL CONSTRUCTED IN 1933 BY
CIVILIAN CONSERVATION CORPS (CCC)

AVERAGE YEARLY
SNOWFALL 400"
ELEVATION 6987

WATER TEMP.
SUMMER 93°
WINTER 112°

▲ *BOILING RIVER: Thousands of gallons of scalding water create a steaming cascade down the banks of the icy river.*

◀ *The surging mixture of hot and cold water among the rocks delivers a dynamic massage.*

#351 BOILING RIVER
In Yellowstone National Park.

A section of Gardiner River which is heated by a large inflow of geothermal water from Boiling Spring. Elevation 5500 ft. Open all year.

Natural Mineral Water at 140 degrees emerges from Boiling Spring at the rate of over 8,000 gallons per minute. When this water flows over the bank into the Gardiner River it creates a turbulent mixture ranging from 70 to 110 degrees. Because of the visibility from a main tourist highway bathing suits are advisable during daylight hours.

No facilities available at the river. Refer to Yellwstone Park map for location of services.

On the North Entrance road, between Mammoth Hot Spring and the town of Gardiner, look for 45th parallel sign on east side of road. Turn into parking area beyond sign and hike ½ mile upstream to confluence of hot and cold water.

► *FIREHOLE RIVER GORGE: Diving from a cliff looks more dangerous than it is.*

▼ *MADISON CAMPGROUND WARM SPRING: Just right for lolling on a warm muddy bottom.*

#352   MADISON CAMPGROUND WARM SPRING
In Yellowstone National Park.

Shallow, mud-bottom soaking pool near the west boundary of Yellowstone Park. Elevation 7000 ft. Open May 1 to October 31.

Natural Mineral Water bubbles up through riverside mud bank at approximately 100 degrees. Volunteers have built a rock dam to create the primitive soaking pool. Because of the proximity to Madison Campground bathing suits are advisable, at least during daylight hours.

No services available at the pool. Refer to Yellowstone Park map for location of services.

To get to pool, park on Loop G in Madison Campground and walk south toward the Firehole River.

#353   FIREHOLE RIVER GORGE
In Yellowstone National Park.

A popular swimming and diving area in a geothermally heated river. Elevation 7000 ft. Open May 1 to October 31.

The Firehole River is warmed to nearly 80 degrees by geothermal water run-off from several active geyser basins. Swimmers like to ride the cascades through a portion of the river canyon, and divers leap from the cliffs into the deeper pools. Bathing suits advisable.

No services available at the gorge. Refer to a Yellowstone Park map for the location of services.

Take "Cascade of the Firehole" drive turnoff just south of Madison Junction in Yellowstone Park. Watch for the gorge on the west side of the one-way road.

#354 MIDWAY GEYSER BASIN
In Yellowstone National Park.

A section of the Firehole River which is heated by a large inflow of geothermal water from the Midway Geyser Basin. Elevation 7000 ft. Open May 1 to November 1.

Natural Mineral Water flows out of the ground in the form of geysers and drains into the Firehole River just above the footbridge joining the parking area to the Midway Geyser Basin. This creates a turbulent mixture ranging from 70 to 110 degrees. Because of the visibility from the bridge, bathing suits are advisable during daylight hours.

Note: Sometimes anti-bathing personnel within the Park Service prevail upon the Superintendent to arbitrarily close this popular site, despite the fact that it is completely legal to bathe in geothermal water once that water has joined with a surface stream. Inquire at a Ranger Station about the current status of bathing in the Firehole River at Midway Geyser Basin Bridge, and, if you find it closed, insist on filing a written complaint against that arbitrary closure.

No services at the bridge. Refer to a Yellowstone Park map for the location of services.

Refer to a Yellowstone Park map to locate the Midway Geyser Basin and the bridge over the Firehole River.

►*MIDWAY GEYSER BASIN: This whole section of the river is heated by the cascade of boiling river down the bank.*

▼*HUCKLEBERRY HOT SPRINGS: This geothermal pool is nearest to Yellowstone.*

#355   HUCKLEBERRY HOT SPRINGS
Box 1049   (307) 543-2402
Jackson, WY 83001   PR + RV

Commercial RV resort operating on leased land within Grand Teton National Park. Elevation 7200 ft. Open June 1 through mid-September.

Natural Mineral Water flows out of the ground at 140 degrees. Outdoor swimming pool is maintained at 80 to 85 degrees. Bathing suits required.

Grocery store, service station, overnight RV spaces and picnic area available on the premises. No credit cards. 1 mile to motel, restaurant, full hook-up RV spaces and public bus.

On US 89, 2 miles south of the Yellowstone National Park South Entrance.

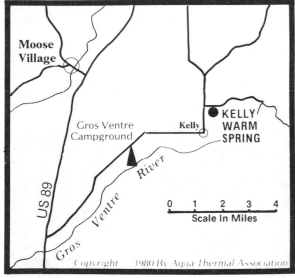

ASTORIA MINERAL HOT SPRINGS

KELLY WARM SPRING: *Large but cool.*

Moose Village

Gros Ventre Campground

Kelly

KELLY WARM SPRING

US 89

Gros Ventre River

0 1 2 3 4
Scale In Miles

Copyright 1980 By Aqua Thermal Association

#356   KELLY WARM SPRING   *(see map)*
In Grand Teton National Park.

Large unimproved pool surrounded by agricultural land east of the Teton peaks.

Natural Mineral Water flows up through gravel bottom into pool at 80 degrees. Highway is only 20 yards away so bathing suits are advisable in the daytime.

No services on the premises. ½ mile to grocery store and service station. 2 miles to campground. 14 miles to motel, restaurant, full hook-up RV spaces and public bus.

Source map: Grand Teton National Park.

#357   ALPENHOF HOTEL
Box 288   (307) 733-3242
Teton Village, WY 83025   Hydrojet Pool   MH

#358   TETON HOT POTS
Box 152   (307) 733-7831
Teton Village, WY 83025   PR

Commercial rent-a-tub establishment in the Jackson business district. Elevation 6200 ft. Open all year.

City water gas-heated. Three wood tubs (2 private, 1 public) maintained at 105 degrees. Two cold plunges (1 private, 1 public) at 50 to 60 degrees. Two saunas (1 private, 1 public). Bathing suits required in public area; not in private rooms.

3 blocks to motel, restaurant, grocery store, service station and public bus. ½ mile to full hook-up RV spaces.

Street address is 365 N. Cache, which is US 89, 3 blocks north of the center of the town of Jackson.

#359   ASTORIA MINERAL HOT SPRINGS
Star Route, Box 18   (307) 733-2659
Jackson, WY 83001   PR + RV

Modern, well kept resort in the Snake River Canyon. Elevation 6100 ft. Open May 1 to October 1.

Natural Mineral Water flows out of the ground at 104 degrees. Outdoor swimming pool (no chlorine) maintained at 84 to 92 degrees. Bathing suits required.

Full hook-up RV spaces, tent spaces, picnic area, grocery store, horse rentals and raft trips available on the premises. 2 miles to motel, restaurant and service station. 17 miles to public bus.

Located on US 26, 17 miles south of the town of Jackson.

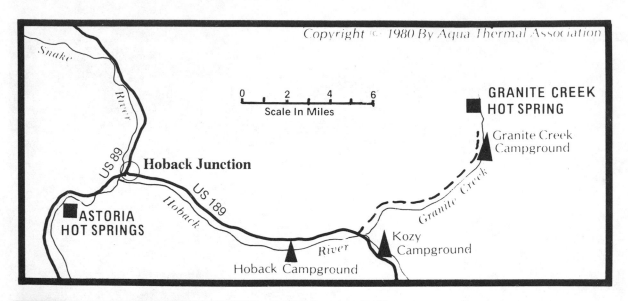

Copyright © 1980 By Aqua Thermal Association
Snake
River
0 2 4 6
Scale In Miles
GRANITE CREEK
HOT SPRING
Granite Creek
Campground
US 89
Hoback Junction
US 189
Hoback
Granite Creek
ASTORIA
HOT SPRINGS
Kozy
Campground
River
Hoback Campground

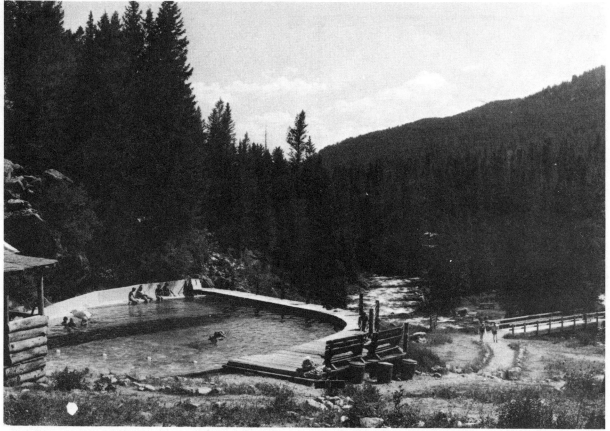

#360 GRANITE CREEK HOT SPRING   (see map)
South of the town of Jackson.

Cement swimming pool at the head of a wooded canyon in Teton National Forest. Day use only, for a fee paid to the operator who holds a lease on the site. Elevation 7000 ft. Open all year.

Natural Mineral Water flows out of the ground at 112 degrees, and has some cold surface water added as needed to control the pool temperature from 105 in winter to 95 in summer. No chlorine added. Bathing suits required.

Picnic area at pool. 1 mile to campground. 10 miles to motel and restaurant. 22 miles to all other services, including public bus.

Source map: Teton National Forest.

#361 SAWMILL LODGE

	(307) 455-2643
DuBois, Wy 92513	Therapy Pool RV

#362 CODY ATHLETIC CLUB
North Fork Star Route   (307) 527-7131
Cody, WY 82414   PR + MH

Fully equipped health club and motel 30 miles east of Yellowstone National Park.

Natural Mineral Water is pumped out of the ground at 87 degrees. Outdoor swimming pool (no chlorine) maintains a temperature of 86 degrees. Gas-heated city water is maintained at 107 degrees in the outdoor jet pool. Men's and women's exercise rooms, each with a sauna. Also a co-ed steam bath. Bathing suits required except in saunas.

Rooms and racquetball courts available on the premises. ½ mile to all other services. 2 miles to public bus.

Located on the north side of US 26, two miles west of the town of Cody.

FOUNTAIN OF YOUTH RV PARK: Where floating on big innertubes is an art.

GRANITE CREEK HOT SPRING: Superb mountain facility near F.S. campground.

CODY ATHLETIC CLUB: Nice motel pools.

#363 PAYNE'S FOUNTAIN OF YOUTH RV PARK
Box 711   (307) 864-9977
Thermopolis, WY 82443   PR + RV

Older RV park with unique mineral water bathing facilities. Elevation 4300 ft. Open all year.

Natural Mineral Water flows out of an artesian well at 130 degrees at a rate of over 1 million gallons per day. A portion of this flow is channeled through a cooling pond into a soaking pool the size of a football field, where the temperature varies from 110 at one end to 100 degrees at the exit end. Bathing suits required in the pool.

Full hook-up RV spaces available on the premises. No credit cards. 2 miles to all other services, including public bus.

Located on US 20, two miles north of the town of Thermopolis.

HOT SPRINGS STATE PARK

This square mile of land, with the Big Spring in the center, was presented to the State of Wyoming by the Federal Government after it had been purchased from the Shoshoni and Arapahoe Indians in 1896. Elevation 4300 ft. Open all year. All of the establishments on the grounds are supplied with natural mineral water from the Big Spring, which flows out of the ground at 135 degrees.

All services not provided by an establishment in the State Park are available within ½ mile, except the public bus, which is 5 miles away.

#364A STATE BATH HOUSE (see map)
State Park (307) 864-9902
Thermopolis, WY 82443

Outdoor soaking pool and indoor soaking pool are maintained at 100 to 104 degrees. Eight indoor individual tubs are controllable up to 105 degrees. All pools use non-chlorinated flow-through mineral water. No charge for pool or tub use. Bathing suits required in soaking pools, not in private rooms. Nominal charge for suit or locker rentals. No credit cards.

#364B TEPEE POOLS (see map)
Box 70 (307) 864-9250
Thermopolis, WY 82443 PR

Outdoor swimming pool - 98 degrees. Indoor swimming pool - 93 degrees. Indoor soaking pool - 105 degrees. Indoor wooden hot tub - 93 degrees. Flow-through mineral water, with no chlorine, used in all pools. Bathing suits required.

Snack bar on the premises. No credit cards.

#364C STAR PLUNGE (see map)
Box 627 (307) 864-3771
Thermopolis, WY 82443 PR

Outdoor swimming pool - 92 to 96. Indoor swimming pool - 96 to 98. Indoor soaking pool - 106 to 108. Outdoor thrill slide and pool - 94 degrees. Indoor steam bath. All pools use flow-through mineral water, without chlorine. Bathing suits required.

Snack bar on the premises. No credit cards.

#364D PLAZA HOTEL AND APARTMENTS (see map)
Box 671 (307) 864-2251
Thermopolis, WY 82443 PR + MH

Older resort building with men's and women's bathhouses. Each bathhouse has 4 individual mineral water tubs and 2 steam baths. Bathing suits not required in bathhouses.

Rooms, massage and sweat wrap are available on the premises. No credit cards.

#364E HOLIDAY INN (see map)
Box 1323 (307) 864-3131
Thermopolis, WY 82443 PR + MH

Conventional motel with men's and women's bathhouses. Each bathhouse has 4 individual mineral water tubs, 2 steam baths and 2 saunas. Outdoor swimming pool, available only to registered guests, contains chlorinated, gas-heated city water, at 78 degrees.

Restaurant and rooms available on the premises. Visa, Master Charge, Diners Club, American Express, Carte Blanche and Gulf credit cards accepted.

#364F GOTTSCHE REHABILITATION CTR. (see map)
Box 790 (307) 864-2147
Thermopolis, WY 82443

This unique center was funded by the Gottsche Foundation, and built alongside the Hot Springs County Memorial Hospital. A wide range of physical, occupational and vocational therapies are offered with medical and psychological services. Doctor's prescription required for admission. Complete information brochure will be sent on request.

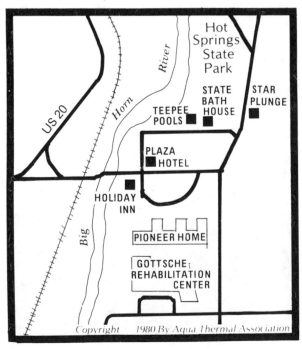

STATE BATH HOUSE: Free outdoor pools.

STAR PLUNGE: Handy poolside snack bar.

TEEPEE POOLS: Spring terraces in background.

#365   CHIEF WASHAKIE PLUNGE
Box 217   (307) 332-2735
Ft. Washakie, WY 82514   PR

Plunge and recreational area operated for and by the Shoshone and Arapahoe Indian Tribes. Non-Indians pay a fee to use the facilities. Elevation 5500 ft. Open all year.

Natural Mineral Water flows out of the ground at 109 degrees. Outdoor swimming pool maintained at 93 to 103 degrees. Nine individual indoor tubs maintained at 103 degrees. Bathing suits required except in private rooms.

Picnic area available on the premises. 4 miles to restaurant, grocery store and service station. 8 miles to full hook-up RV spaces. 16 miles to motel and public bus.

On US 287, in the town of Ft. Washakie, look for Hines General Store, then follow signs 3 miles east to plunge.

CHEIF WASHAKIE PLUNGE: A modern style resort emphasizing recreational use of mineral water rather than therapeutic.

#366A   HOBO POOL
In the town of Saratoga.

An improved but unfenced soaking pool, plus a fenced municipal swimming pool, on the edge of town in rolling ranch country. Elevation 6800 ft. Open all year.

Natural Mineral Water flows out of the source spring at 115 degrees. Large outdoor soaking pool (no charge) maintains a temperature of 100 to 110, and volunteers have channeled the soaking pool run-off into shallow rock pools along the edge of the North Platte River. Daily charge is made for use of the swimming pool, which is maintained at 90 degrees. Bathing suits required.

Picnic area available at the pools. 3 blocks to motel, restaurant, grocery store and service station. ½ mile to full hook-up RV spaces. 40 miles to public bus.

Watch for HOBO POOL sign on Wyoming Route 130 in the town of Saratoga, then follow signs 4 blocks to pool.

#366B   THE SARATOGA INN
Box 867   (307) 326-5261
Saratoga, WY 82331   MH

Golf and tennis resort surrounded by rolling ranch country. Elevation 6800 ft. Open all year.

Natural Mineral Water is pumped out of the ground at 114 degrees. Outdoor swimming pool is maintained at approximately 100 degrees. Bathing suits required.

Rooms, restaurant, golf and tennis available on the premises. Visa, Master Charge and American Express accepted. 4 blocks to grocery store and service station. 1 mile to full hook-up RV spaces. 40 miles to public bus.

From Wyoming Route 130 in the town of Saratoga, go east on Bridge street and follow signs 4 blocks to resort.

#367   BEST WESTERN HITCHING POST INN
1600 West Lincoln Way   (307) 638-3301
Cheyenne, WY 82001   Therapy Pools   MH

#368   HOLIDAY INN
2009 S. Hwy. 59   (307) 686-3000
Gillette, WY 82716   Whirlpool   MH

THE TOWN OF SARATOGA IS
NOT RESPONSIBLE FOR
ACCIDENTS IN THE HOBO POOL
OR SWIMMING POOL AREA
—SARATOGA TOWN COUNCIL—

POOL RULES
NO ALCOHOL WITHIN 100
YARDS
NO DOGS IN THE POOL AREA
NO OVERNIGHT CAMPING
PROPER SWIMMING ATTIRE
REQUIRED
RESPECT THE RIGHTS OF
OTHERS
TOWN COUNCIL

◆ *HOBO POOL: City-maintained cement pool. Primitive rock & sand pool 40 years ago.*

▶ *THE SARATOGA INN: This resort wants people to stay out of the pool at night.*

POOL CLOSED
FROM 1030 PM/9 AM
FOR HEAVY
CHLORINATION
FOR INN GUESTS
AND
MEMBERS ONLY
CARDS WILL BE
CHECKED

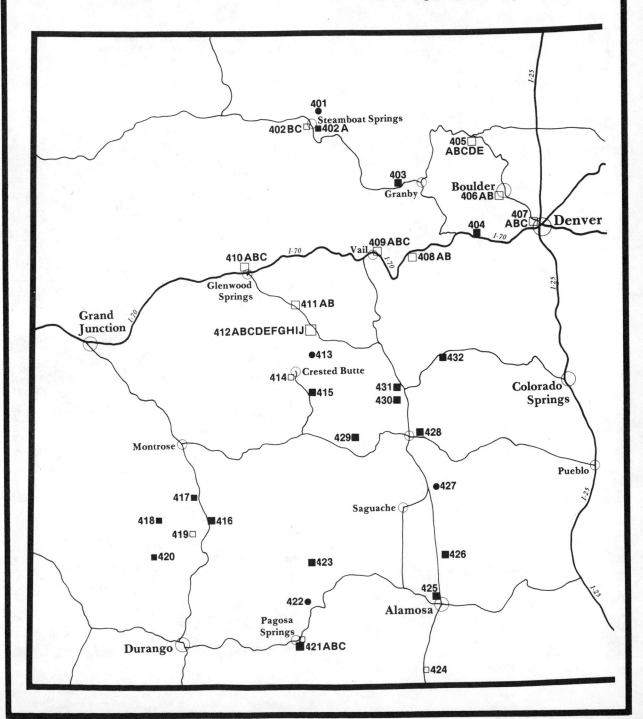

● Unimproved Mineral Water Locations
■ Improved Mineral Water Locations
□ City Water Establishments

REGIONAL KEY MAP

Each location has been assigned a
location number, and Directory listings
have been arranged numerically.

401
Steamboat Springs
402BC ■402 A
405
ABCDE
403
Granby
Boulder
406AB
407
ABC
Denver
404
409ABC
Vail
410ABC
408 AB
Glenwood
Springs
411AB
Grand
Junction
412ABCDEFGHIJ
●413
414 Crested Butte
432
415
431
430
Colorado
Springs
429
428
Montrose
Pueblo
●427
417
Saguache
418■ ■416
419□
426
420
423
425
422●
Pagosa
Springs
Alamosa
Durango
421ABC
424

COLORADO:

Colorful, Commercial and Conflicted

The flatlands of eastern Colorado, like the eastern counties of Montana, simply have no hot springs. All the geothermal activity is found in the western mountains, which are at least colorful, and often stupendous. This means that every hot spring is close to tourist attractions such as fishing, hunting, skiing, hiking. As a result, nearly every sizeable hot spring has long since been developed into some form of commercial resort, a few of them dating back 100 years. There are only two accessible publicly-owned undeveloped hot springs, and both of them (Conundrum and Wolf Creek Pass) require strenuous hikes or cross-country skiing into remote sections of National Forest land.

A few larger resorts have managed to modernize to meet changing public demands. Glenwood Springs Lodge no longer offers therapeutic cures but rather emphasizes recreation and a Health Club for improving physical fitness. This shift in policy and facilities, together with a good location on an Interstate Highway, has enabled Glenwood Springs to remain open and busy. Some of the more remote hot spring sites were initially developed as guest ranches, rather than therapy spas, so they have also continued to prosper, with hot mineral water serving as an added attraction rather than the main attraction.

On the other hand, the smaller therapy-

GLENWOOD SPRINGS LODGE . . . . page 129

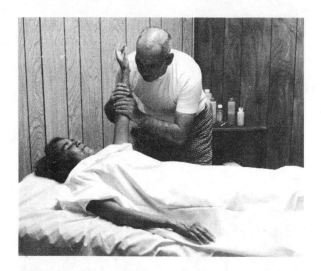

WIESBADEN RESORT . . . . page 132

oriented resorts have seen their clientele get older and more scarce each year, and are uncertain how to attract younger customers. Without the benefit of that old hot mineral water mystique, they have difficulty competing with newer and better located ski resorts.

Changing public attitudes toward clothing are responsible for another conflict involving hot springs. Back in the 1960s hippies camped and skinny-dipped at small undeveloped hot springs such as South Canyon, near the town of Glenwood Springs. By the 1970s the hippies were joined by other people who preferred to take hot mineral baths in the nude. This created a dilemma for the town, which owns the South Canyon property. There was no interest in developing a new hot spring resort to compete with the resorts in Glenwood Springs, and civic indignation smoldered over the skinny-dipping shenanigans in South Canyon, yet no agency was anxious to tackle the task of keeping people away from such an attractive nuisance. In 1979, after much hesitation and hand-wringing, the city ordered all pools, pipes, dams, shelters, etc. removed from South

Canyon in an effort to render the site totally unattractive and useless. Within a few weeks the bootleg rebuilding process started up again, leaving the town in an ongoing struggle to destroy faster than the hot spring enthusiasts can build.

A similar conflict has been plaguing the town of Steamboat Springs, where the non-profit Steamboat Springs Health and Recreation Association was given the Strawberry Park hot springs property many years ago "for the public good." The Association already operates a large swimming and soaking pool complex at an historic hot spring in the city of Steamboat Springs, and has never been interested in developing Strawberry Park, which is 10 miles out of town on a steep gravel road. The Association has often posted "No Nude Bathing" signs at Strawberry Park, only to have them promptly torn down. Conventional families have complained about nude bathers, but no one had the time or money to attempt enforcement of the NO NUDE BATHING signs. In 1979, a newly-elected sheriff decided to clear up the problem by leading a posse on an anti-nudity raid, whcih resulted in a dozen arrests. The offenders were found guilty of indecent exposure and then given a sentence of cleaning up the court house and the littered area by the

STRAWBERRY PARK HOT SPRINGS . . page 124

122

springs. However, there was also quite a controversy over whether such a raid was an appropriate use of Sheriff's deputies, in view of other more serious law enforcement problems in the county. So the raids have stopped, at least temporarily, the wary skinny-dippers have returned, and the complaints about nudity at Strawberry Park have resumed. As of the beginning of 1980 the Steamboat Springs Health and Recreation Association has decided to sell the Strawberry Park property "for the public good,"

The clothing policy conflicts involving public hot springs occasionally have some parallels among privately-owned hot pools, especially the ski resorts which cater to a younger clientele. At some locations, in the late hours, the official policy requiring bathing suits is unofficially ignored. Discreet inquiries are advisable, because only the official policy will appear in the resort brochure.

A few hot spring resort owners have resolved the conflict by flatly adopting some form of clothing-optional policy. At Valley View Hot Springs, which has a membership structure rather than being open to the public, clothing is optional anywhere on the exensive grounds. There is also a long waiting list for membership.

Gas-heated city water hot pools are beginning to appear in Colorado, and more are expected. At Sunshine's Paradise, in Crested Butte, the official policy in the single co-ed soaking pool is "bathing suits are welcome," but few customers bother to bring one. At Time Out Baths, in Boulder, each of the five wooden hot tubs occupies a private room or a private roof patio, so each couple or group that rents a tub can adopt their own clothing policy. Also, during daytime hours, one of the tubs is designated as a clothing-optional communal co-ed hot pool, handy for single customers who do not want to rent a whole room and pool by themselves.

Geothermal Energy

The resort buildings at Wiesbaden and Waunita Hot Springs have been geothermally heated for years. In the town of Pagosa Springs, privately drilled wells have been supplying geothermal energy for heating several residences and commercial buildings. A DOE-funded demonstration project, coordinated by a Pagosa city-county-school board advisory committee, has been initiated to design, construct and monitor a downtown heating district, using some of the existing wells, and drilling more as needed for future expansion.

DOE-funded studies have also been started on a district heating project in Idaho Springs and an agriculture processing plant in San Luis Valley.

The following codes were used
in the preparation of listings
and maps on the following pages.

NATURAL MINERAL WATER LOCATIONS ARE SET IN BOLD TYPE — like this
GAS HEATED CITY WATER LOCATIONS ARE SET IN REGULAR TYPE — like this

---

PR = Tubs or pools for rent, by hour, day or treatment.
MH = Rooms or cabins for rent by day, week or month.
RV = Vehicle spaces for rent by day, week, month, or year.

Open all year means that there are no doors or gates closed during a part of the year. However, snow or high water may temporarily make the location inaccessible.

———— Paved highway
– — — — Gravel or dirt road
·············· Hiking trail
▲ Campground

STRAWBERRY PARK HOT SPRINGS:
Limited parking is only 20 ft. away.
Skinny-dippers choose to risk arrest.
Clothing is optional, even for a massage.

#401 STRAWBERRY PARK HOT SPRINGS
Near the town of Steamboat Springs

Undeveloped group of hot springs surrounded by Routt National Forest. Elevation 7500 ft. Open all year.

Natural Mineral Water flows out of many openings at more than 165 degrees, gradually cooling as it runs toward a cold stream. Volunteers have built many shallow rock and log pools in which hot and cold water mix to provide a wide choice of temperatures. Controversy and confusion surround the question of clothing policy. Unless official positions have changed, bathing suits are advisable during daylight hours at least.

No services available on the premises. 7 miles of steep gravel road to all services in the town of Steamboat Springs.

Inquire at Routt National Forest Ranger Station about directions, road conditions and clothing policy before trying to reach this location.

124

#402A STEAMBOAT SPRINGS HEALTH & RECREATION
Box 1211   (307) 879-1828
Steamboat Springs, CO 80477   PR

Community plunge, hot pool and sauna on the edge of town. Elevation 6700 ft. Open all year except swimming pool open only May through November.

Natural Mineral Water flows out of the ground at 104 degrees. Large outdoor swimming pool maintained at 85 degrees. Enclosed soaking pool · 99 degrees. Separate men's and women's sauna rooms. Bathing suits required except in saunas.

Picnic area available on the premises. 2 blocks to motel, restaurant, grocery store and service station. 1 mile to full hook-up RV spaces and public bus.

Located on north side of US 40 on the west edge of the town of Steamboat Springs.

#402 RAMADA INN
Box 388   (303) 879-2900
Steamboat Springs, CO 80477   Whirlpool   MH

#402C STORM MEADOWS TOWNHOUSE RESORT
Box AAA   (303) 879-1035
Steamboat Springs, CO 80477   Therapy Pool   MH

STEAMBOAT SPRINGS HEALTH & REC.: HOT SULPHUR SPRINGS: Hot & swim pools.

#403 HOT SULPHUR SPRINGS
Box 175   (303) 725-3306
Hot Sulphur Springs, CO 80451   MH

Older resort on a main road through the Rocky Mountains. Elevation 7600 ft. Open April to November 1.

Natural Mineral Water flows out of the ground at 115 degrees. Outdoor swimming pool is maintained at 85 degrees. Outdoor soaking pool · 100 degrees. Two indoor soaking pools in private rooms rented by the hour. Two indoor soaking pools in separate men's and women's bathhouses. Indoor pools controllable to 110 degrees. Bathing suits required except in indoor pools.

Rooms, tent spaces and picnic area available on the premises. No credit cards. 3 blocks to restaurant, grocery store, service station and public bus. 75 miles to full hook-up RV spaces.

From US 40 in the town of Hot Sulphur Springs, follow signs across river to resort.

INDIAN SPRINGS RESORT: One of the largest indoor pools with translucent roof.

#404 INDIAN SPRINGS RESORT
Box 1300   (303) 623-2050
Idaho Springs, CO 80452   PR + RV + MH

Large older resort surrounded by Arapahoe National Forest. Elevation 7300 ft. Open all year.

Natural Mineral Water flows out of the ground at 124 degrees. One indoor swimming pool (translucent roof) maintained at 90 degrees. Seven soaking pools in separate men's and women's tunnels · 104 to 114 degrees. Six individual tubs in private rooms, controllable to 108 degrees. Bathing suits required in swimming pool area; prohibited in soaking pools.

Rooms, restaurant, massage. Full hook-up RV spaces and picnic area available on the premises. VISA and Mastercharge accepted. 2 blocks to grocery store and service station. 1 mile to campground. 4 miles to public bus.

From Interstate 70, take Idaho Springs exit to business district, then follow signs south on Soda Springs Road to resort.

125

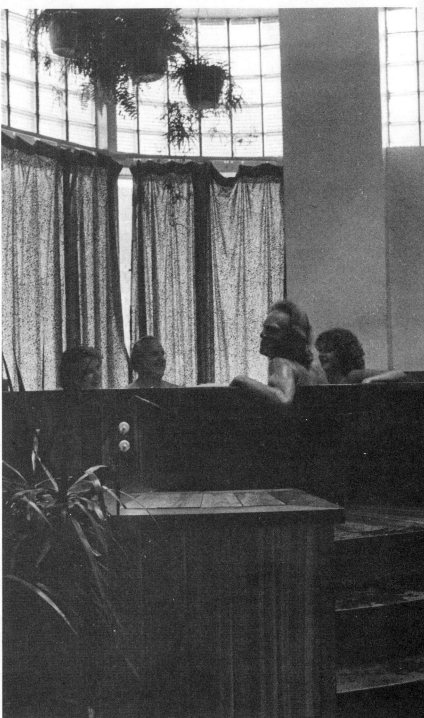

 TIME OUT BATHS: *Photos of the outdoor sign and indoor communal hot tub at this pioneering rent-a-tub establishment.*

▲ *This roof-top hot tub has been designated as a women-only communal tub during the day. After 7PM it will rent to private parties.*

#405A   TYROL MOTOR INN
1240 Big Thompson Ave.
Estes Park, CO 80517
(303) 586-3382
Therapy Pool   MH

#405B   LANE GUEST RANCH
Box 1766C
Estes Park, CO 80517
(303) 747-2493
Therapy Pool   MH

#405C   HOLIDAY INN
Box 1468
Estes Park, CO 80517
(303) 586-2332
Whirlpool   MH

#405D   CARIBOU CHALET
1700 Big Thompson Canyon Rd.
Estes Park, CO 80517
(303) 586-2358
Therapy Pool   MH

#405E   BEST WESTERN LAKE ESTES MOTOR INN
Box 1466
Estes Park, CO 80517
(303) 586-3386
Therapy Pool   MH

#406A   TIME OUT BATHS
805 Pearl St.
Boulder, CO 80302
(303) 442-TUBS

Unique rent-a-tub establishment in the town of Boulder. Elevation 6000 ft. Open all year.

Gas-heated city water. Three rooftop redwood tubs in private patios, and two indoor cedar tubs in private rooms. Temperatures - 102 to 108. Tubs available by the hour, half-hour, communal, group rate or monthly rate. Bathing suits optional in all tubs.

Massage and saunas available on the premises. 1 block to restaurant, grocery store and service station. 1 miles to motel. 5 miles to public bus. 15 miles to full hook-up RV spaces.

From US 36, west on Colorado Route 119 to 9th St., then north to Pearl, and west to 805.

#406B   BEST WESTERN BOULDER INN
770 28th St.
Boulder, CO 80303
(303) 449-3800
Therapy Pool   MH

#407A   MARRIOTT HOTEL
I-25 at Hampden Ave.
Denver, CO 80222
(303) 758-7000
Whirlpool   MH

#407B   BRONCO INN
110 W. 104th Ave.
Northglenn, CO 80234
(303) 451-1234
Therapy Pool   MH

#407C   ROYAL INN
3270 Youngfield St.
Wheat Ridge, CO 80033
(303) 238-7701
Therapy Pool   MH

#408A   LAKE DILLON CONDOTEL
Box 308
Lake Dillon, CO 80435
(303) 468-2409
Therapy Pool   MH

#408B   RAMADA INN - SILVERTHORNE
Box 368
Silverthorne, CO 80498
(303) 468-6200
Whirlpool   MH

#409A   ANTLERS/LIONS HEAD CONDOMINIUMS
Box 280
Vail, CO 81567
(303) 476-2471
Hydrojet Pool   MH

#409B   VAIL ATHLETIC CLUB HOTEL
Box 573
Vail, CO 81657
(303) 476-0700
Therapy Pool   MH

#409C   VAIL INTERNATIONAL CONDOMINIUMS
Box 877
Vail, CO 81657
(303) 476-0111
Hydrojet Pool   MH

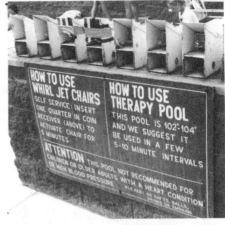

▲ GLENWOOD HOT SPRINGS LODGE: Coin-operated therapy chairs.

◀ Indoor jet pool in Health Club.

▼ This is one of the largest active hot springs resorts in the West.

#410A   GLENWOOD HOT SPRINGS LODGE
Box 308   (303) 945-6571
Glenwood Springs, CO 81601   PR + MH

Very large resort across from the train depot in the center of town. Elevation 5700 ft. Open all year.

Natural Mineral Water flows from the ground at 130 degrees. Huge outdoor swimming pool maintained at 98 degrees. Outdoor soaking pool with jet chairs - 104 degrees. Indoor jet pool (in Athletic Club) - 102 degrees. Steam bath and sauna in Athletic Club. Bathing suits required.

Rooms and restaurant on the premises. VISA, Mastercharge, American Express, Diner Club and Carte Blanche accepted. 3 blocks to grocery store, service station and public bus. 3 miles to full hook-up RV spaces.

See Glenwood city map for directions.

#410B   GLENWOOD SPRINGS VAPOR CAVES
709 E. 6th   (303) 945-5825
Glenwood Springs, CO 81601

Small health center 1 block from the large Hot Springs Resort complex. Elevation 5700 ft. Open all year.

Natural Mineral Water and steam emerge directly into two steam bath caves (separate men's and women's). Bathing suits not required in caves.

Facials and massages are available on the premises. No credit cards. 3 blocks to motel, restaurant, grocery store, service station and public bus. 3 miles to full hook-up RV spaces.

See Glenwood City map for directions.

#410C   HEALTH SPA
Box 536   (303) 945-5021
Glenwood Springs, CO 81601   PR

Chiropractic office and bathhouse portion of old resort. Elevation 5700 ft. Open all year.

Natural Mineral Water flows out through two springs at 110 and 124 degrees. Six individual tubs in private rooms controllable up to 112 degrees. Bathing suits not required in tubs.

Chiropractic adjustment and massage available on the premises. No credit cards. ½ mile to motel, restaurant, grocery store, service station and public bus. 3 miles to full hook-up RV spaces.

See Glenwood City map for directions.

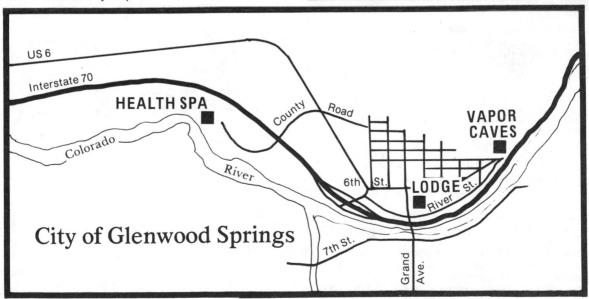

#411A   INNS AT SNOWMASS
Box B-2   (303) 923-4310
Snowmass Village, CO 81615   Therapy Pool   MH

#411B   TIMBERLINE LODGE & CONDOMINIUMS
Box I-2   (303) 933-4000
Snowmass Village, CO 81615   Therapy Pool   MH

#412A   GLORY HOLE LODGE
Box 617   (303) 925-6760
Aspen, CO 81611   Hydrojet Pool   MH

#412B   HIGHLANDS INN
Box 4708   (303) 925-5050
Aspen, CO 81611   Therapy Pool   MH

#412C   LIMELIGHT LODGE
228 E. Cooper   (303) 925-3025
Aspen, CO 81611   Hydrotherapy Pool   MH

#412D   POMEGRANATE INN
Box 1368   (303) 925-2700
Aspen, CO 81611   Therapy Pool   MH

#412E   ASPEN CHATEAUX APARTMENTS
Original & Durant St.   (303) 925-1100
Aspen, CO 81611   Hydrojet Pool   MH

#412F   ASPEN CHATEAUX CONDOMIMIUMS
Box 4949   (303) 925-1400
Aspen, CO 81611   Hydrojet Pool   MH

#412G   BOOMERANGE LODGE
500 W. Hopkins   (303) 925-3416
Aspen, CO 81611   Whirlpool   MH

#412H   CHRISTMAS INN
232 W. Main & 2nd St.   (303) 925-3822
Aspen, CO 81611   Whirlpool   MH

#412I   THE CRESTWOOD
Box 5460   (303) 923-2450
Aspen, CO 81615   Therapy Pool   MH

#412J   THE GANT CONDOMIMIUMS
Ute Ave. & West End St.   (303) 925-5000
Aspen, CO 81611   Whirlpool   MH

#413   CONUNDRUM HOT SPRINGS
In the White River National Forest south of the town of Aspen.

Two primitive pools surrounded by spectacular Rocky Mountain scenery. Elevation 11,200 ft. Open from June 1 to September 15.

Natural Mineral Water flows out of the ground at 100 degrees, supplying two primitive rock pools. The local custom is clothing optional.

No services on the premises. 8 miles of trail and 5 miles of rough road to a campground. 20 miles to all other services, including public bus.

Obtain directions, instructions and information about current trail conditions at a White River National Forest Ranger Station before attempting to reach this site.

#414   SUNSHINE'S PARADISE
401 1st St.   (303) 349-6563
Crested Butte, CO 81224   PR

Very informal bathhouse in funky old building on side street of quaint old mining town. Elevation 8900 ft. Open all year.

Gas heated city water. One communal indoor jet pool made of natural rock - 105 degrees. Adjoining cold pool - 60-70 degrees. Sauna, shower, soap, shampoo, towels and use of hair dryer included in single fee. Bathing suits welcome but not required.

Massage available on the premises. 2 blocks to restaurant, grocery store, motel and service station. 7 miles to campground with tent spaces. 32 miles to full hook-up RV spaces and public bus.

From the town of Gunnison, on US 50, take Colorado Route 135 north 28 miles to Crested Butte.

◀ *SUNSHINE'S PARADISE: This old mining town cabin has a natural rock jet pool.*

◀ *At one end of the hot pool there is even a natural rock cold pool for the brave ones.*

▶ *Sunshine herself minds the store in this combination entry, office and dressing room.*

#415   CEMENT CREEK RANCH

Crested Butte, CO 81224

(303) 349-5541

Rustic Guest Ranch in wooded mountain canyon, surrounded by Gunnison National Forest. Elevation 9500 ft. Open May to November.

Natural Mineral Water flows out of the ground at 78 degrees into outdoor swimming pool (no chlorine), maintaining a temperature of 70-75 degrees. Bathing suits required.

Cabins, meals, saddle horses, etc. available on the premises to registered guests, for a minimum of one week, by prior reservation only. No credit cards. 13 miles to restaurant, grocery store and service station. 17 miles to full hook-up RV spaces. 27 miles to public bus.

From the town of Gunnison, on US 50, take Colorado Route 135 north 20 miles. Follow signs to resort.

#416 WIESBADEN MOTEL AND HEALTH RESORT

Box 349   (303) 325-4347
Ouray, CO 81427   PR + MH

Modern resort surrounded by Uncompahgre National Forest. Elevation 7700 ft. Open all year.

Natural Mineral Water flows from two springs at 111 and 117 degrees. Outdoor swimming pool (no chlorine) maintained at 80-90 degrees. Indoor soaking pool (no chlorine) · 106 degrees. Sauna with 117 degree pool in sauna room. Bathing suits required. Geothermal heat in all buildings.

Rooms, picnic area, massage, reflexology, facials and exercise equipment available on the premises. VISA and Mastercharge accepted. 2 blocks to restaurant, grocery store and service station and public bus. 6 blocks to full hook-up RV spaces.

Located in the town of Ouray, on US 550, 74 miles north of Durango.

#417 LOPA HOT SPRINGS

Rte. 1   (303) 626-5505
Ridgway, CO 81432

Small hydrotherapy center. Elevation 6900 ft. Open all year.

Natural Mineral Water flows out of the ground at 132 degrees. Seven individual indoor tubs, with whirlpool units, are controllable up to 105 degrees. Bathing suits not required in individual rooms.

Massage and GNO therapy available on the premises. No credit cards. All services, including public bus, available within 1 mile.

Located on US 550, 1 miles south of the town of Ridgway.

LOPA HOT SPRINGS: A therapy-oriented treatment center in the high country area.

WEISBADEN MOTEL & HEALTH RESORT: Full size chlorine-free swimming pool.

Soaking pool was hewed out of bedrock.

#418   GUTHRIE PARK WARM SPRING
Box 26   (303) 728-3710
Placerville, CO 81430

Small soaking tub in an old mining tunnel. Elevation 7500 ft. Open all year.

Natural Mineral Water flows out of the ground at 87 degrees into small tub, which is rented by the hour. Clothing optional.

Cabins available on the premises. No credit cards. 3 blocks to grocery store and service station. 3 miles to restaurant and full hook-up RV spaces. 21 miles to public bus.

Located on Colorado Rte 145, across the river from the Placerville store. Inquire for Stella at the big white house.

#419   TELLURIDE LODGE
Box 127   (303) 728-3881
Telluride, CO 81435   Therapy Pool   MH

#420   DUNTON HOT SPRINGS
Dunton Route   (no phone)
Dolores, CO 81323   PR + MH

Historic old resort surrounded by San Juan National Forest. Elevation 8800 ft. Open May to mid-November.

Natural Mineral Water flows out of the ground at 107 degrees. One indoor soaking pool maintains a temperature of 104 to 106 degrees, and is rented by the hour with prior reservation. Bathing suits not required in soaking pool building.

Rooms and restaurant available on the premises. No credit cards. 2 miles to campground. 16 miles to service station and full hook-up RV spaces. 24 miles to grocery store. 45 miles to public bus.

From the town of Dolores, go 13 miles northeast on Colorado Route 145, then 22 miles (gravel) on West Dolores Road (National Forest Access Road).

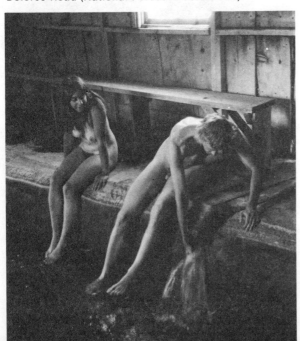

#421A   THE SPA
Box 37   (303) 264-5910
Pagosa Springs, CO 81147   PR

Older spa and motel on south bank of San Juan River. Elevation 7100 ft. Open all year.

Natural Mineral Water flows out of the ground at 156 degrees. Outdoor swimming pool (no chlorine) for motel guests only, maintained at a temperature of 85 degrees. **Two indoor soaking pools, in men's and women's bathhouses, held to 108 degrees.** Bathing suits required except in bathhouses.

Rooms available on the premises. VISA and Mastercharge accepted. All other services available within 10 blocks.

Location visible from Colorado Route 160 in the town of Pagosa Springs. Follow signs across bridge.

▲▼ *THE SPA: The sign on the bathhouse says, HOT BATHS, and that is what you get.*

The minimum is 108; some days it is higher.

◄ *DUNTON HOT SPRINGS: This single large pool, in its own building, is drained daily.*

PLEASE
IHR. LIMIT
108° TEMP
Bathe 5 Min. or Less
USE HAND RAIL
NO SOAP IN POOL
NO SHORTS IN POOL
SHOWER

PAGOSA HOT SPRING: Hot mineral water flows over the bank and across this mud flat. A peaceful wallow in the warm ooze suddenly escalated into this hilarious mud fight, followed by a swim in the river.

#421B PAGOSA HOT SPRING
In the town of Pagosa Springs.

Non-commercial unimproved flow of hot water into the San Juan River. Elevation 7100 ft. Open all year.

Natural Mineral Water flows out of the ground at 156 degrees. A part of the large output emerges from a colorful mineral formation in front of the Pagosa Inn and flows across a small mud flat into the river. Volunteers occasionally build shallow rock pools near the river to soak in the hot muddy water. Because of high visibility, bathing suits are advisable.

No services available on the premises. All services available within 10 blocks.

The location is visible from Colorado Route 160 in the town of Pagosa Springs.

#421C BEST WESTERN PAGOSA LODGE
Box 245   (303) 968-2271
Pagosa Springs, CO 81147   Whirlpool   MH

#422 WOLF CREEK PASS HOT SPRINGS
In the Weminuche Wilderness Area northeast of the town of Pagosa Springs.

Two primitive springs on the West Fork of the San Juan River, seven miles by trail from the West Fork trailhead. Elevation 10,000 ft. Difficult access during high water and snow seasons.

Natural Mineral Water flows out of the ground at 100 degrees into shallow rock pools at the edge of the stream. The local custom is clothing optional.

No services on the premises. 7 miles to campground. 26 miles to all other services, including public bus.

Obtain directions and information on current trail conditions from a Rio Grande National Forest Ranger Station before attempting to reach this site.

#423 4UR GUEST RANCH
Box 340   (303) 658-2202
Creede, CO 81130

Modern De Luxe Guest Ranch surrounded by Rio Grande National Forest. Elevation 8,400 ft. Open June 1 to November 15.

Natural Mineral Water flows out of the ground at 140 degrees. Outdoor swimming pool maintained at 78 degrees. Indoor jet pool (no chlorine) maintained at 110 degrees. Bathing suits required.

Guest Ranch services, including rooms, meals, horses, tennis, etc. available on the premises for a minimum stay of one week, by prior reservation only. No credit cards. ½ mile to service station. 4 miles to full hook-up RV spaces. 9 miles to grocery store. 15 miles to public bus.

From the town of South Fork on US 160, take Colorado Route 149 northwest 22 miles to Wagon Wheel Gap. 100 yards past old railroad station, follow signs two miles south to resort.

#424 KOA CAMPGROUND - CONEJOS RIVER
                                      (303) 376-2255
Antonito, CO 81120   Therapy Pool   RV

#425 JONES SPLASHLAND
Box J   (303) 589-5151
Alamosa, CO 81101   PR

Large rural community plunge. Elevation 7500 ft. Open May through September.

Natural Mineral Water flows out of the ground at 106 degrees. Outdoor swimming pool is maintained at 87-88 degrees. Bathing suits required.

Snack bar on the premises. No credit cards. Two miles to motel, cafe, grocery store and service station. 5 miles to all other services including public bus.

On Colorado Route 17, two miles north of the town of Alamosa.

#426 SAND DUNES (HOOPER) HOT SPRING
Box 43   (303) 378-2424
Hooper, CO 81136

Wholesale fish farm near Great Sand Dunes National Monument. Elevation 8000 ft. Visitors by prior arrangement only.

Natural Mineral Water flows out of artesian well at 118 degrees, directed by pipes and valves into tanks and ponds where catfish are grown. The facilities include a cement swimming pool no longer approved for public use.

No services available on the premises. 25 miles to all other services.

▲ 4UR GUEST RANCH: *A trampoline is one of the several extras available at 4UR.*

▲ JONES SPLASHLAND: *A local teenager demonstrates one of the diving boards.*

▼ SAND DUNES HOT SPRING: *Tons of fish grow in dozens of these tanks and ponds.*

▶ *VALLEY VIEW HOT SPRINGS: This is the largest of the natural bottom pools.*

◀ *The upper pools are especially peaceful at dawn. (See also back cover of book)*

#427 VALLEY VIEW HOT SPRINGS
Box 175   *(no phone)*
Villa Grove, CO 81155

Semi-commercial membership resort on the western slope of the Sangre De Cristo Range. Elevation 8,700 ft. Open all year.

Natural Mineral Water flows out of several different springs at temperatures of 80 to 105 degrees. Outdoor natural-bottom swimming pool maintained at 89 degrees. Seven other primitive rock soaking pools vary in temperature from 85 to 105 degrees. A small sauna building includes an 83 degree pool. Bathings suits optional anywhere on the grounds.

Rustic unfurnished cabins and tent spaces available on the premises to members and their guests. Write first for permission to visit and/or get on the membership waiting list. No credit cards. 12 miles to restaurant, grocery store, service station and public bus. 15 miles to full hook-up RV spaces.

At the junction of US 285 and Colorado Route 17 take the gravel road due east 7 miles to end of road.

136

Some special photographs from the
family albums of Valley View members:

▲ This couple devised a truly relaxed
backgammon game. (Tim Murray photo)

◄ The view from the upper springs
includes the mountains as well as
the big valley below. (Murray photo)

► During winter months, steam from
the hot pools condenses on the
surrounding bushes, creating crystal
white decorations. (Murray photo)

▼ The completion of this large new
concrete swimming pool in 1979 led
to a week-long grand opening
celebration. (Neil Seitz photo)

SALIDA HOT SPRING: This diver is really prepared for deep water.

A bond issue was being considered to expand and modernize these facilities.

WAUNITA HOT SPRINGS RANCH: Experimental fish ponds in foreground.

#428   SALIDA HOT SPRINGS
Rainbow Blvd.   (303) 539-6738
Salida, CO 81201   PR + RV

Municipal plunge, hot baths, park and playground. Elevation 7000 ft. Open Memorial Day to Labor Day.

Natural Mineral Water is piped from Poncha Springs and arrives at 114 degrees. Outdoor swimming pool is maintained at 85 degrees. Outdoor soaking pool - 100 degrees. Six individual indoor tubs, controllable to 110 degrees. Bathing suits required except in tubs.

Overnight RV spaces and picnic grounds available on the premises. No credit cards. 1 block to cafe, motel, grocery store and service station. 1 mile to full hook-up RV spaces and public bus.

Located on US 50, 6 miles east of junction with US 285.

#429   WAUNITA HOT SPRINGS RANCH
Rte. 2, Box 56E   (303) 641-1266
Gunnison, CO 81230   MH

Older guest ranch, surrounded by Gunnison National Forest. Elevation 9000 ft. Open all year.

Natural Mineral Water flows out of the ground at 175 degrees. Outdoor swimming pool maintained at 95 degrees. Bathing suits required. Geothermal heat in all buildings.

Guest Ranch services, including rooms, meals, saddle horses, fishing, etc. available on the premises to registered guests. Minimum stay of three days by prior reservation only. 15 miles to grocery store, service station and campground. 28 miles to full hook-up RV spaces and public bus.

On US 50, go 19 miles east from the town of Gunnison, then follow signs 8 miles north to ranch.

#430   MOUNT PRINCETON HOT SPRINGS

Nathrop, CO 81236

(303) 395-2361

PR + MH

Large modern resort surrounded by San Isabel National Forest. Elevation 8500 ft. Open to the public from Memorial Day to Labor Day. Group reservations accepted Labor Day to Memorial Day.

Natural Mineral Water flows out of the ground at 132 degrees. Odorless and tasteless, this water is used in all pipes, including those which water the lawns. Outdoor swimming pool maintained at 85 degrees. Soaking pool (for lodge guests only) maintained at 95 degrees. Six individual indoor tubs, controllable to 110 degrees. Bathing suits required except in individual rooms.

Rooms, restaurant and picnic area available on the premises. No credit cards. 5 miles to all other services including public bus.

From US 285, in Nathrop, go west 5 miles on Colorado Route 162 to resort.

#431   JUMP STEADY RESORT

Rte. 1, Box 203 State Hwy 306
Buena Vista, CO 81211

(303) 395-8605

MH

Small motel resort being expanded to include pools. Phone for status of construction. Elevation 8900 ft. Open all year.

Natural Mineral Water flows out of the ground at 119 degrees, and is piped to all rooms, where individual tubs may be controlled up to 115 degrees. Bathing suits not required in rooms.

Rooms available on the premises. VISA and Master-charge accepted. 6 miles to all other services, including public bus.

From US 24, in Buena Vista, go 5½ miles west on Colorado Route 306.

#432   HARTSEL HOT SPRINGS

East of Buena Vista, in the South Platte River valley.

Tattered remains of a small bathhouse enterprise. Main buildings vandalized and deteriorating. Elevation 9300 ft. Open all year.

Natural Mineral Water flows out of the ground at 130 degrees. Tiny shack with old bathtub has been built over the spring, and each use requires filling the tub with bucketsful of water lifted from the spring. Bathing suit not required in the shack.

No services available on the premises. 1 mile to services in the town of Hartsel.

At the intersection of US 24 and Colorado Route 9, the buildings are visible 200 yards south.

MOUNT PRINCETON HOT SPRINGS: The shallow end of this high country pool has plenty of room for families.

HARTSEL HOT SPRINGS: The tiny shack is the only useable building left.

139

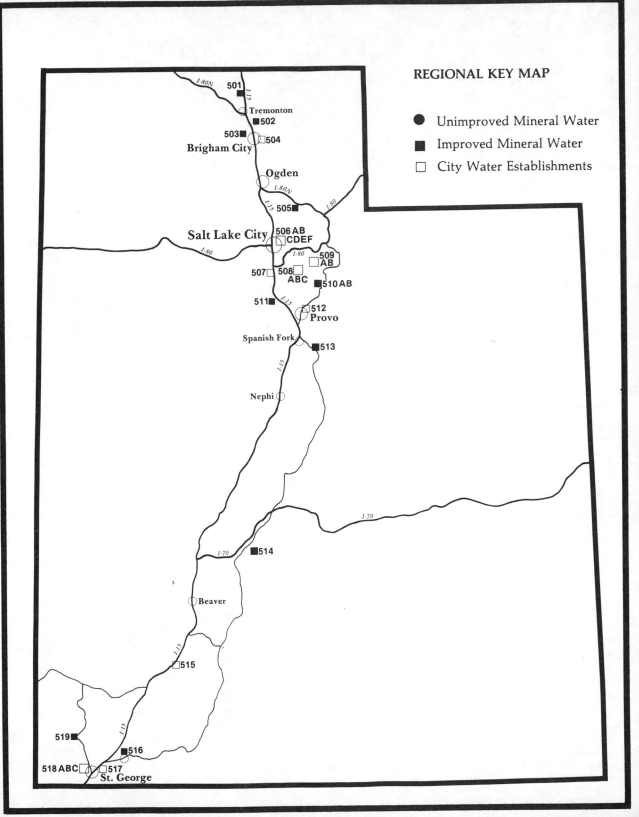

REGIONAL KEY MAP

● Unimproved Mineral Water

■ Improved Mineral Water

□ City Water Establishments

501

Tremonton

502

503 □ 504

Brigham City

Ogden

I-80N

I-15 505

Salt Lake City 506 AB
CDEF

I-80

509
AB

507 508
ABC

510 AB

511

512
Provo

Spanish Fork

513

Nephi

I-70

I-70 514

Beaver

I-15 515

519

516

518 ABC 517

St. George

UTAH:

Where Rock is In and Skinny-Dipping is Out

By a quirk of geology, all of Utah's dozen hot springs are strung out in a north-south line which parallels the route of Interstate 15. All of them have been commercially developed at one time or other so there are no publicly-owned primitive hot spring sites in the state. However, a couple of them have gone through a complete cycle of development, growth, popularity, decline, closing, and sometimes total destruction. The trash-littered end products of such a cycle may be unposted and available to the public, but they can hardly be called idyllic.

There are no skinny-dipping pools in Utah, officially or unofficially. One of the residents explained it this way, "In Utah, most of the people go by what the Church of Jesus Christ of Latter Day Saints says. That's the Mormon Church, which strongly states the belief that exposure of the nude human body is sinful, and therefore condemned. Now, if the Mormon Church says that is so, you had better believe it. Or, if you don't believe it, you had better, while you are in Utah, act as though you did believe it." That is good advice.

Most Utah hot spring sites are basically community plunges, with large swimming pools, picnic grounds, snack bar, and sometimes more elaborate amusement park devices. Most, but not all, swimming pools are continuously serenaded by the local rock

PAH TEMPE HOT SPRINGS . . . . page 152

and roll station through speakers mounted on the roof of the snack bar. These are primarily action-oriented summer resorts, with the hot springs providing a low-cost source of heating for the water in the swimming pool and the slide pool. Individual or communal soaking pools, with a temperature of over 100 degrees, are seldom part of the available facilities.

Pah Tempe Mineral Springs is in a class by itself. Each hour thousands of gallons of 108 degree sulphur water pour out of the walls of the Virgin River Canyon, while thousands more gallons bubble up through the sandy bottom of the river. Soaking pools have been carved into the cliffs, and a conventional swimming pool is also available. Pah Tempe is a favorite with families in the summer because the kids have so much fun running around in the shallow river water and under the hot waterfalls along the bank. Don't forget to bring your bathing suit, and keep it on.

142

Geothermal Energy

Because nearly all Utah hot spring resorts are open only from Memorial Day to Labor Day, geothermal space heating has never been considered worthwhile within those resorts. However, three DOE-funded projects are under way to demonstrate the application of geothermal energy to institutional, agricultural, and urban situations.

The Utah State Prison project involves drilling a new well designed to provide geothermal energy for space heating, and culinary water heating in the minimum security block. The design will also include the potential for expansion into all the prison buildings.

A three acre greenhouse specializing in growing roses is the target of the agricultural demonstration project.

The heating district demonstration project at the city of Monroe contains several unique features. Production wells will be drilled on property belonging to Monroe Hot Springs, under an agreement which guarantees the resort an adequate flow of hot mineral water if the drilled wells decrease the flow from the existing hot springs. The high mineral content of the thermal water makes it impractical to pipe it directly into the heat exchangers at the high school, city hall, fire station, and other buildings included in the first phase of the project. Instead, a single large heat exchanger near the well site will transfer heat into a closed city-water system which will circulate to the various target buildings.

A smaller version of this heat exchanger has been in use at Monroe Hot Springs Resort for years. The mineral water could not be used in the swimming pool because the addition of chlorine caused it to turn black. Therefore, city water is used, and it is heated by being pumped through a series of pipes immersed in a flow-through tank of hot mineral water.

The following codes were used in the preparation of listings and maps on the following pages.

NATURAL MINERAL WATER LOCATIONS ARE SET IN BOLD TYPE — like this
GAS HEATED CITY WATER LOCATIONS ARE SET IN REGULAR TYPE — like this

PR = Tubs or pools for rent, by hour, day or treatment.
MH = Rooms or cabins for rent by day, week or month.
RV = Vehicle spaces for rent by day, week, month, or year.

Open all year means that there are no doors or gates closed during a part of the year. However, snow or high water may temporarily make the location inaccessible.

——————	**Paved highway**
– — — —	**Gravel or dirt road**
··············	**Hiking trail**
▲	**Campground**

▲ BELMONT SPRINGS: Newly built facilities, such as this slide-equipped swim pool are changing the capabilities of this resort.

◄ Some of the natural mineral pools are dangerous as well as hot.

► This newly-drilled artesian well flows pressurized hot mineral water.

▼ This largest of the natural-bottom soaking pools was often used by the Indians who inhabited the territory before the arrival of white men.

#501 BELMONT SPRINGS

Plymouth, UT 84330

(801) 458-3200
PR + RV

Expanding new commercial resort in open rolling country north of the Great Salt Lake. Phone for current status of construction. Elevation 4300 ft. Open April through September.

Natural Mineral Water flows out of artesian well at 131 degrees, and out of springs at 85 degrees. Temperatures are controlled by mixing water reaching various pools. One outdoor swimming pool (with R & R music) temperature controlled between 92 and 108 degrees depending on the season. Outdoor soaking pool maintained at 95 degrees. Outdoor jet pool maintained at 100 to 110 degrees. Outdoor gravel-bottom soaking pool flows at 106 degrees. Bathing suits required.

Full hook-up RV spaces, 9 hole golf course, tennis courts, and picnic area available on the premises. No credit cards. 7 miles to motel, cafe, grocery store and service station. 11 miles to public bus.

On Interstate 15, 1 mile south of the town of Plymouth. Follow signs.

#502 CRYSTAL HOT SPRINGS
Route 1
Honeyville, UT 84314

(801) 279-8104

Historic resort with spacious tree-shaded grounds and world's largest side-by-side hot and cold springs. Pools and facilities are being totally remodeled by new owner. Phone for status of construction. Elevation 4700 ft. Open all year.

Natural Mineral Water flows out of the ground at 135 degrees. Multiple outdoor and indoor pools are in the construction plans. Bathing suits will be required in the outdoor pools.

Contruction plans include full hook-up RV spaces, picnic areas and restaurant. 10 miles or less to all other services, including public bus.

On Utah Route 69, 2½ miles north of the Honeyville exit from Interstate 15.

#503 STINKY SPRINGS
Near the town of Brigham City

A small, partially vandalized cement block bathhouse alongside a highway in the flat country north of the Great Salt Lake. Elevation 4000 ft. Open all year.

Natural Mineral Water flows out of the ground at 118 degrees, through a culvert under the highway, and into three cement soaking pits in the abandoned building. Temperature is controlled by diverting the flow of 118 degree water as desired. If you can close your eyes to the trash, and close your nose to the sulphur dioxide smell, it is possible to appreciate the water.

From Interstate 15, take the Golden Spike Exit and go west 9 miles on Utah Route 83. Bathhouse is on south side of highway.

#504 RED BARON MOTEL
1167 S. Main St.
Brigham City, UT 84302

(801) 723-8511
Whirlpool MH

▲ *CRYSTAL HOT SPRINGS: The separate outflows from the hot and cold springs join together in the center of the photograph.*

▼ *STINKY SPRINGS: This derelict may not have class but it does have character.*

145

▲ COMO SPRINGS RESORT: *Typical summer-season plunge with snack bar and dressing rooms.*

#505   COMO SPRINGS RESORT
Box 386   **(801) 829-3489**
Morgan, UT 84050   **PR + RV + MH**

Older rural plunge and recreation park in the foothills northeast of Salt Lake City. Elevation 5000 ft. Open Memorial Day to Labor Day.

Natural Mineral Water flows out of the ground at 82 degrees. Outdoor swimming pool (with R & R music) is maintained at 78 degrees. Same temperature in separate slide pool. Bathing suits required.

Cabins, restaurant, picnic grounds and full hook-up RV spaces available on the premises. No credit cards. 1 mile to grocery store and service station. 25 miles to public bus.

From Interstate 80N take Morgan exit and follow signs to resort.

#506A   BEST WESTERN LITTLE AMERICA MOTEL
500 S. Main St.   (801) 363-6781
Salt Lake City, UT 86101   Whirlpool   MH

#506B   BEST WESTERN WORLD MOTOR HOTEL
1900 S. State St.   (801) 487-7806
Salt Lake City, UT 84115   Hydrojet Pool   MH

#506C   HOLIDAY INN - DOWNTOWN
230 W. 6th St.   (801) 532-7000
Salt Lake City, UT 84101   Whirlpool   MH

#506D   INTERNATIONAL DUNES HOTEL
206 SW Temple St.   (801) 521-9500
Salt Lake City, UT 84101   Therapy Pool   MH

#506E   RAMADA INN
999 S. Main St.   (801) 531-7200
Salt Lake City, UT 84111   Hydrojet Pool   MH

#506F   SALT LAKE HILTON
150 W. Fifth St.   (801) 532-3344
Salt Lake City, UT 84101   Therapy Pools   MH

#506G   TRAVELODGE AT SIXTH SOUTH TOWER
161 W. 600th St. S.   (801) 521-7373
Salt Lake City, UT 84101   Hydrojet Pool   MH

#507   BEST WESTERN SANDMAN INN
380 W. 72nd St.   (801) 561-2256
Midvale, UT 84047   Therapy Pool   MH

#508A   SNOWBIRD LODGES
Snowbird   (801) 742-2000
Alta, UT 84070   Hot soaking pool   MH

#508B   RUSTLER LODGE
State 210   (801) 742-2200
Alta, UT 84070   Hydrojet Pool   MH

#508C   ALTA SKI LODGE
State 210 Little Cottonwood Canyon   (801) 742-3500
Alta, UT 84070   Hydrojet Pool   MH

#509A   BLUE CHURCH LODGE & ANNEX
Box 1720   (801) 649-8009
Park City, UT 84060   Hydrojet Pool   MH

#509B   PROSPECTOR SQUARE SKI CENTER
Box 1698   (801) 649-7100
Park City, UT 84060   Hydrapool   MH

▲ *THE HOMESTEAD: Indoor and outdoor pools (under construction) are visible in to the left of the main resort building.*

▶ *A hot soaking pool with hydrojets will adjoin the new indoor swimming pool. The many windows admit much sunlight.*

#510A   THE HOMESTEAD
700 N. Homestead Drive   (801) 654-1102
Midway, UT 84049   PR + RV + MH

Remodeled historic resort with new pools, spacious tree-shaded lawns, indoor and outdoor dining with deluxe service, specializing in family reunions and group meetings. Elevation 5600 ft. Open all year.

Natural Mineral Water flows out of the ground at 98 degrees, into the outdoor soaking pool, outdoor wooden hot tub and the indoor jet pool. Indoor and outdoor swimming pools will contain gas-heated city water. Phone for information concerning the temperature of these newly constructed pools. Bathing suits required.

Rooms, restaurant, overnight RV spaces, tennis courts, and saddle horses available on the premises. VISA and Mastercharge accepted. 1 mile to grocery store and service station. 6 miles to full hook-up RV spaces and public bus.

From US 189 in Charleston, take Utah Route 113 to Midway and follow signs to resort.

MOUNTAIN SPA RESORT: Back when the west was wild this resort got a wide-open reputation. Today the outdoor and indoor pools are operated to attract families.

#510B   MOUNTAIN SPAA RESORT
800 North 200 East   (801) 654-0721
Midway, UT 84049   PR + RV + MH

Historic older resort formerly known as Luke's Hot Pots, includes some 100 year old buildings. Elevation 5700 ft. Open from April to October, except mineral baths are open all year.

Natural Mineral Water flows out of the ground at 104 degrees. Outdoor swimming pool maintained at 80 to 95 degrees depending on weather. Indoor swimming pool maintained at 90 degrees. Indoor soaking pool averages 103 degrees. Bathing suits required except in soaking pool room.

Rooms, restaurant and full hook-up RV spaces available on the premises. 8 blocks to grocery store and service station. 3 miles to public bus.

From US 189 in Charleston, take Utah Route 113 to Midway. Take River Road to 600 north, follow signs to 200 east.

#511   SARATOGA RESORT
Saratoga Road at Utah Lake   (801) 768-8206
Lehi, UT 84043   PR + RV

Lakeside recreation resort, with picnic grounds, rides, concessions and boat launching facilities. Elevation 4200 ft. Open Memorial Day to Labor Day.

Natural Mineral Water flows and is pumped out of the ground at 120 degrees. Two outdoor swimming pools (with R & R music), one diving pool, and two slide & splash pools, all maintained at 90 degrees. Bathing suits required.

Restaurant, picnic ground and overnight RV spaces available on the premises. No credit cards. 7 miles to all other services, including public bus.

From the town of Lehi, go west on Utah Route 72 to street 9500 West; follow signs south to resort.

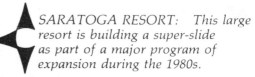

SARATOGA RESORT: This large resort is building a super-slide as part of a major program of expansion during the 1980s.

Red Sandstone Hotel

CASTILLA HOT SPRING:

 According to these old photos this was once a truly major resort.

Today there is no trace of any buildings except this battered cement block house built over the spring.

The shallow puddle is a far cry from the elegance of the original plunge.

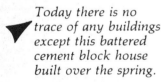

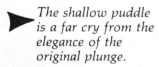

◄ MONROE HOT SPRINGS: *Due to the high mineral content of the hot water, city water must be used in the swim pool and the jet pool. The heat exchanger and mineral water soaking pool are visible on hill behind the swim & jet pools.*

▼ *The view from the hillside soaking pool includes the town of Monroe, where a demonstration project is under way to provide geothermal heat to all buildings.*

#512   ROYAL INN
55 E. 1230
N. Provo, UT 84601

(801) 373-0800
Whirlpool   MH

#513   CASTILLA HOT SPRING
Near the town of Spanish Fork.

Partially vandalized cement hut built over source spring of historic old resort. The structures are all gone, but plenty of litter remains. Elevation 4000 ft. Open all year.

Natural Mineral Water flows directly into hut at 104 degrees, maintaining a shallow soaking pool at that temperature. Bathing suits advisable during daytime as area is clearly visible from the highway.

No services on the premises except for some parking areas sprinkled with broken glass. 9 miles to all services, including public bus.

On the north side of US 6, 3½ miles west of the town of Thistle.

#514   MONROE HOT SPRINGS
Box B
Monroe, UT 84754

(801) 527-4014
PR + RV

RV park with swimming pool and hillside soaking pool overlooking an agricultural valley. Elevation 5500 ft. Open all year, except swimming pool open only from Memorial Day to Labor Day.

Natural Mineral Water flows out of the ground at 135 degrees into reservoir and heat exchanger, then into hillside soaking pool, which maintains a temperature between 100 and 105 degrees. The city water in the outdoor swimming pool and jet pool (with R & R music) is heated by the mineral water in the heat exchanger to an average of 80 degrees. Bathing suits required. Indoor soaking pools and a grotto steam bath are planned. Inquire about the status of construction.

Full hook-up RV spaces and picnic area available on the premises. All other services, including public bus, available within 9 blocks.

On Utah Route 118, 5 miles east of Interstate 70 (US 89).

#515   CHALET VILLAGE
Box 488
Parowan, UT 84761

(801) 586-6778
Therapy Pool   MH

▼ *VEYO RESORT: In addition to this pool and snack bar Veyo has a volleyball court.*

▲ *PAH TEMPE HOT MINERAL SPRING: Soaking pools have been carved in the cliff.*

#516   PAH TEMPE HOT MINERAL SPRINGS
Box 946   **(801) 635-2879**
Hurricane, UT 84737   **PR + RV + MH**

A unique resort with a spectacularly large flow of hot sulphur water out of the sides of the Virgin River Canyon and up from the bottom of the river bed. Elevation 3000 ft. Open all year.

Natural Mineral Water flows out of many openings at 105 to 108 degrees. Outdoor swimming pool is maintained at 100 to 105 degrees. Four soaking pool grottos carved from the cliff hold water at 107 degrees. Jet pools, some with pyramid covers, average 106 degrees. Bathing suits required at all times. No smoking or drinking around pools.

Cabins and overnight RV spaces available on the premises. No credit cards. ½ mile to cafe, grocery store and service station. 1 mile to full hook-up RV spaces and public bus.

On Utah Route 9, two miles north of Hurricane. Follow signs to resort.

#517   SUNDOWNER INN
Box 280   **(801) 673-3537**
Washington, UT 84780   *Hydrojet Pool   MH*

#518A   WESTON'S LAMPLIGHTER MOTEL
460 E. 100 St. St. George Blvd.   **(801) 673-4861**
St. George, UT 84770   *Therapy Pool   MH*

#518B   TRAVELODGE - DOWNTOWN
60 W. St. George Blvd.   **(801) 673-4666**
St. George, UT 84770   *Therapy Pool   MH*

#518C   BEST WESTERN CORAL HILLS MOTEL
125 E. St. George Blvd.   **(801) 673-4844**
St. George, UT 84770   *Therapy Pool   MH*

#519   VEYO RESORT
Veyo Star Route Box 107   **(801) 628-0124**
Central, UT 84722   **PR + RV**

Older rural plunge and picnic park with a small running stream. Elevation 4600 ft. Open March 15 to September 15.

Natural Mineral Water flows from artesian well at 98 degrees. Outdoor swimming pool (with R & R music) maintains a temperature of 85 degrees. Bathing suits required.

Cafe, overnight RV spaces and picnic area available on the premises. No credit cards. 1 mile to grocery store and service station. 6 miles to motel. 12 miles to full hook-up RV spaces. 18 miles to public bus.

On Utah Route 18, 18 miles north of St. George. Follow signs.

▲ PAH TEMPE MINERAL SPRING:
The swimsuit rules are definite.

▶ One of the soaking pools is out
on the edge of the cliff.

◀ Another pool is tucked into a
grotto carved out of bedrock.

▼ An irresistable attraction is
the gentle battering to be had
under this sulphur water shower.

Alphabetical Master Index

This index includes all of the hot springs we investigated. Key map location numbers and page numbers are given for the springs described in the preceding Directory Section. The designation NUBP (Not Useable By the Public) identifies those sites which are presently inaccessible or non-operational.

When we started our field research we tried to determine the history of all the sites, especially those which had been commercially operated at one time but were no more. However, we learned that some places had been defunct for so many years that no one clearly remembered what did happen. In other cases we asked four different people and got four different answers, none of them readily verifiable. Eventually, we concluded that the only significant fact, for the purpose of this book, was that a specific site was no longer useable, regardless of the reasons. We decided to let the historians speculate about what happened at those places where we *can't* go; we concentrated on what is presently happening at the places where we *can* go.

Some of the hot spring closures are permanent, such as when the spring is drowned under a reservoir created by a new dam. However, most of the non-operational sites do have the potential for reactivation, at the discretion of present or future owners. Burned-down buildings could be replaced, condemned pools could be rebuilt, or a new well could be drilled to increase water flow. Some new hot pools may come into existence as a by-product of geothermal energy projects involving space heating, green houses, or alcohol distillation. We expect to see many changes in the next decade.

This book reports what we found as of the beginning of 1980. If you become aware of later and/or revised information please share it with us by writing to Directory Editor, Aqua Thermal Association, Box 841, Van Nuys, CA 91408. Thank you for helping us make our future publications more accurate.

▲ BURGDORF HOT SPRINGS: The signs
tell us that this pool was closed
to the public by order of the Health Dept.

▼ CORWIN HOT SPRINGS: Economic
factors closed this resort decades ago.

Name	Key Map Location # or Nearby Town	State	Page
CASTILLA HOT SPRING	513	UT	151
CEILANN HOT SPRING	206	ID	50
CEMENT CREEK RANCH	415	CO	131
CHALLIS HOT SPRINGS	246	ID	82
CHAMBERLAIN HOT SPRINGS	Villa Grove	CO	NUBP
CHATANOOGA HOT SPRINGS	242B	ID	78
CHICO HOT SPRINGS LODGE	316	MT	104
CHIEF WASHAKIE PLUNGE	365	WY	118
CLARENDON HOT SPRINGS	Hailey	ID	NUBP
CODY ATHLETIC CLUB	362	WY	115
COLGATE HOT SPRINGS	Lowell	ID	NUBP
COMO SPRINGS RESORT	505	UT	146
CONUMDRUM HOT SPRING	413	CO	130
COTTONWOOD HOT SPRINGS	Buena Vista	CO	NUBP
CORWIN SPRINGS	Gardiner	MT	NUBP
COUGAR RESERVOIR (CAPRA) HOT SPRING	169	OR	35
COVE SWIMMING POOL	179	OR	40
CRANE HOT SPRING	Crane	OR	NUBP
CRYSTAL SPRINGS	502	UT	145
DAUGHERTY'S HOT SPRING	Glen's Ferry	ID	NUBP
DEL RIO HOT SPRINGS	262	ID	92
DOWNATTA HOT SPRINGS	261	ID	92
DUNTON HOT SPRINGS	420	CO	133
DUTCH FRANK'S HOT SPRINGS	241C	ID	77
EASLEY WARM SPRINGS	(Omitted by request of owner.)		
EAST LAKE HOT SPRINGS	La Pine	OR	NUBP
ELKHORN HOT SPRINGS	312	MT	102
ELLSWORTH HOT SPRINGS	Carey	ID	NUBP
FAIRMONT HOT SPRINGS RESORT	310	MT	102
FIREHOLE RIVER GORGE	353	WY	111
FOLEY SPRINGS	McKenzie Bridge	OR	NUBP
FOUNTAIN OF YOUTH RV PARK	363	WY	115
4UR GUEST RANCH	423	CO	135
FRAZIER HOT SPRING	Bridge	ID	NUBP
GIVENS HOT SPRINGS	226	ID	64
GLENWOOD HOT SPRINGS LODGE	410A	CO	129
GLENWOOD SPRINGS VAPOR CAVES	410B	CO	129
GOLD FORK HOT SPRINGS	209	ID	52
GOLDMEYER HOT SPRINGS	Snoqualmie	WA	NUBP
GOTTSCHE REHABILITATION CENTER	364F	WY	116
GRANITE CREEK HOT SPRING	360	WY	115
GRANTSVILLE WARM SPRINGS	Grantsville	UT	NUBP
GREAT NORTHERN HOT SPRINGS	Scenic	WA	NUBP
GREEN CANYON HOT SPRINGS	256	ID	89
GUS ALLEN'S HOT SPRING	Lakeview	OR	NUBP
GUTHRIE PARK WARM SPRING	418	CO	133
GUYER HOT SPRINGS	Ketchum	ID	NUBP

Name	Key Map Location # or Nearby Town	State	Page
HAAGA HOT SPRINGS	241B	ID	77
HAILEY HOT SPRINGS	Hailey	ID	NUBP
HART MOUNTAIN HOT SPRING	184	OR	42
HARTSEL HOT SPRINGS	432	CO	139
HAVEN LODGE	219	ID	60
HEALTH SPA	410C	CO	129
HEISE HOT SPRINGS	255	ID	88
HIDEAWAY SPRINGS	La Grande	OR	NUBP
HILLBROOK NURSING HOME	319	MT	105
HIPPY DIP HOT SPRINGS	Glenwood Springs	CO	NUBP
HOBO POOL	366A	WY	118
HOLIDAY INN	364E	WY	116
HOME HOTEL AND MOTEL	259B	ID	91
THE HOMESTEAD	510A	UT	147
HOOPER (SAND DUNES) HOT SPRINGS	426	CO	135
HOOPER (SODA) SPRINGS	260	ID	91
HORSE CREEK HOT SPRING	250	ID	85
HOT LAKE	La Grande	OR	NUBP
THE HOT SPOT	252	ID	87
HOT SPRINGS CAMPGROUND	217	ID	60
HOT SPRINGS LANDING AT MAGIC RESERVOIR	233	ID	70
HOT SULPHUR SPRINGS	Susanville	OR	NUBP
HOT SULPHUR SPRINGS	403	CO	125
HUCKLEBERRY HOT SPRINGS	355	WY	112
HUNTER'S HOT SPRINGS	Livingston	MT	NUBP
HUNTER'S LODGE	185	OR	43

▲ *MEDICINE SPRINGS:* *This resort was closed when a nearby lumber mill shut down and most of the people moved away.*

▼ *LEHMAN HOT SPRINGS:* *The facilities are used by the owner and his friends while they are waiting for the property to be sold to a new owner/operator.*

Name	Key Map Location # or Nearby Town	State	Page
INDIAN BATHTUB	227	ID	64
INDIAN SPRINGS NATATORIUM	258	ID	89
INDIAN SPRINGS RESORT	404	CO	125
IRON SPRING	Rico	CO	NUBP
JACKSON HOT SPRINGS	165	OR	30
JACKSON HOT SPRINGS LODGE	311	MT	102
JERRY JOHNSON'S HOT SPRINGS	202	ID	49
JONES SPLASHLAND	425	CO	135
JOSEPH'S HOT SPRINGS	Joseph	UT	NUBP
JUMP STEADY RESORT	431	CO	139
JUNIPER HOT SPRING	Craig	CO	NUBP
KAH-NEE-TA VACATION RESORT VILLAGE	172	OR	36
KELLY WARM SPRINGS	356	WY	113
KEM HOT SPRING	243	ID	80
KENNEDY HOT SPRING	102	WA	22
KIRKHAM HOT SPRINGS	220	ID	61
KITSON SPRINGS	Oakridge	OR	NUBP
LA DUKE HOT SPRING	Gardiner	MT	NUBP
LAUREL HOT SPRINGS	207	ID	51
LAVA HOT SPRINGS RESORT	259A	ID	91
LEHMAN HOT SPRINGS	La Grande	OR	NUBP
LEO HANK'S HOT SPRINGS	Lakeview	OR	NUBP
LESTER HOT SPRINGS	Greenwater	WA	NUBP
LIDY HOT SPRINGS	Dubois	ID	NUBP
LOFTUS HOT SPRING	240C	ID	76
LOLO HOT SPRING RESORT	307	MT	100
LOPA HOT SPRINGS	417	CO	132

Name	Key Map Location # or Nearby Town	State	Page
LOST TRAIL HOT SPRING	(Omitted by request of owner.)		
LUCE HOT SPRING	Riverside	OR	NUBP
MADISON CAMPGROUND WARM SPRING	352	WY	111
MANCONDO HOT SPRING	Anaconda	MT	NUBP
McCREDIE HOT SPRINGS	167	OR	32
MEDICAL SPRINGS	Baker	OR	NUBP
MEDICINE HOT SPRINGS RESORT	309	MT	101
MEDITATION POOL (WALL CREEK) HOT SPRING	168	OR	33
MIDDLE FORK HOT SPRINGS	247	ID	82
MIDWAY GEYSER BASIN	354	WY	112
MIRACLE HOT SPRINGS	231	ID	69
MITCHELL BUTTE HOT SPRINGS	Owyhee	OR	NUBP
MOFFETT'S HOT SPRING RESORT	113	WA	25
MOLLY'S HOT SPRING	211	ID	54
MONROE HOT SPRINGS	514	UT	151
MOON DIPPER HOT SPRINGS	213B	ID	57
MT. PRINCETON HOT SPRINGS	430	CO	139
MOUNTAIN SPAA RESORT	510B	UT	148
NAT SOO PAH NOT SPRINGS	232	ID	69
NEAL HOT SPRING	Vale	OR	NUBP
NEW BILTMORE HOT SPRING	313	MT	102
NINEMEYER HOT SPRINGS	241A	ID	77
OGDEN HOT SPRINGS	Ogden	UT	NUBP
OHANAPECOSH HOT SPRING	Mt. Ranier	WA	NUBP
OLYMPIC HOT SPRINGS	109	WA	23
OREGON HOT SPRINGS	Bonanza	OR	NUBP

LIDY HOT SPRINGS: The hot mineral water now supplies only the animal pens since a big snow storm crushed the indoor pool building in the late 1960s.

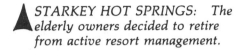

▲ STARKEY HOT SPRINGS: The elderly owners decided to retire from active resort management.

◀ PARADISE HOT SPRINGS: These owners decided to sell shares.

◀ PINKERTON HOT SPRING: A highway buried this hot spring.

▼ WASATCH WARM SPRINGS: The Salt Lake City Recreation Dept. closed this plunge in the 1970s.

159